Abolitionist Leadership in Schools

Abolitionist Leadership in Schools offers school and district leaders rich insights and approaches for recreating, restructuring, and reorienting their service to students, families, staff, and communities in crisis. Though often associated with sudden, large-scale disruptions, crises are ongoing matters—particularly among systemically-oppressed people—that underscore the planning voids, resource inequities, marginalizing policies, and strategic lapses of any teaching and learning community while perpetuating students' social-emotional, psychological, and pedagogical traumas. This expansive book guides school leaders to provide pre-emptive, premeditated, and progressive leadership while countering the impacts of racism that endure in our schools. Working from an abolitionist lineage, author Robert S. Harvey's radically humane vision explores lessons from our collective national past, provides strategic planning with creativities and contingencies, and fosters liberatory decision-making through accountability, communication, and more.

Dr. Robert S. Harvey is Superintendent of East Harlem Scholars Academies, a community-based network of public charter schools in New York City, and Chief Academic Officer of East Harlem Tutorial Program, where he manages an Out-of-School Time program and Teaching Residency. An educator, community broker, and public voice, he has written and spoken extensively on education, race, and intersectional justice; serves on education and arts boards across the country; and is Visiting Professor in the Practice of Public Leadership at the Memphis Theological Seminary.

Abolitionist Leadership in Schools

Undoing Systemic Injustice Through Communally Conscious Education

Robert S. Harvey

NEW YORK AND LONDON

First published 2021
by Routledge
52 Vanderbilt Avenue, New York, NY 10017

and by Routledge
2 Park Square, Milton Park, Abingdon, Oxon, OX14 4RN

Routledge is an imprint of the Taylor & Francis Group, an informa business

Library of Congress Cataloging-in-Publication Data
Names: Harvey, Robert S. (Educator), author.
Title: Abolitionist leadership in schools : undoing systemic injustice through communally conscious education / Robert S. Harvey.
Description: New York, NY: Routledge, 2021. |
Includes bibliographical references. |
Identifiers: LCCN 2020049245 (print) | LCCN 2020049246 (ebook) |
ISBN 9780367679279 (hardcover) | ISBN 9780367679286 (paperback) |
ISBN 9781003133414 (ebook)
Subjects: LCSH: Educational equalization—United States. |
Community and school—United States. |
Social justice and education—United States. |
Discrimination in education—United States.
Classification: LCC LC213.2 .H394 2021 (print) |
LCC LC213.2 (ebook) | DDC 379.2/6—dc23
LC record available at https://lccn.loc.gov/2020049245
LC ebook record available at https://lccn.loc.gov/2020049246

ISBN: 978-0-367-67927-9 (hbk)
ISBN: 978-0-367-67928-6 (pbk)
ISBN: 978-1-003-13341-4 (ebk)

Typeset in Palatino
by codeMantra

Meet the Author

Dr. Robert S. Harvey is an educator, community connector, and systems leader pursuing a vision of justice, equity, and love and devoted to making education a civic priority.

Dr. Harvey is Superintendent of East Harlem Scholars Academies, a community-based network of public charter schools in New York City, and Chief Academic Officer of East Harlem Tutorial Program, where he manages an Out-of-School Time (OST) program and Teaching Residency. He is also Visiting Professor in the Practice of Public Leadership at the Memphis Theological Seminary.

Prior to East Harlem, he served as Head of School for Star Academy College Preparatory in Memphis, Tennessee. Before Memphis, he was Chief Operating Officer/Vice President and Senior Lecturer in Religion and the Social Sciences at Simmons College of Kentucky, an historically Black college in Louisville, Kentucky. Earlier in his career, he worked in Independent day and boarding schools as faculty, director of enrollment, and dean of students.

Dr. Harvey has committed himself to lifelong learning and public intellectualism through a doctorate in leadership, culture, and society from Memphis Theological Seminary, a master of theological studies from Harvard University, and a bachelor of arts from Bryant University. He has also completed executive programs in organizational change and school management from Emeritus Institute and Harvard Graduate School of Education.

His written work has appeared in Education Week, Education Post, Citizen Education, TheGrio, Blavity, Chalkbeat, Education Dive, St. Louis Post-Dispatch, and a variety of academic publications including *Inquiries Journal, The African American Lectionary*, and the *Journal of Unitarian Universalist History*. In addition to his professional and academic commitments, he serves on a variety of nonprofit boards impacting education, mental health, and the arts.

Contents

Acknowledgments

Gratitude is a vulnerable act, isn't it? Finding words to our gratitude is even more vulnerable of a thing, but necessary. Gratitude is the aroma of living well because gratitude rejects the assumption that we have arrived where we are alone. Gratitude is awareness and confession that the mystery of our arrival is only grounded in and guided by community—a community that has moved us closer to our truest and highest self. Who I am today and who I am in writing this book exist only because of the human and sacred relationships for which I am deeply grateful, and moved to the peak of emotions.

Relationships that have invited me to be vulnerable and truthful.
Relationships that have ushered me to new understandings of the world.
Relationships that have partnered with me in paying the price of freedom.

In this world where freedom is costly—and very few people want to pay the price for themselves, and certainly not for others—the relationships in my life have supported me in paying the price to be free.

Freedom is a struggle, not a gift.
Freedom is divine, not human.
One day we decide to be free, and the struggle begins.
The path of that struggle is littered with naysayers.
But in the deep woods, there are angels waiting to help and to guide.
And in the deepest woods, there are ancestors, the wise ones, who ground us.

Of those who have been the brightest and boldest teachers along this struggle, it is the women in my life who have given me the courage to discover, to trust, to fail, to mature, to confess, to deconstruct, to reimagine, and to become. I resist the urge of assuming that this is an adequate expanse to justly and honorably acknowledge the many who have given to this journey. Too many to name. I hold them in my soul and give thanks. But this work and these ideas are shaped by those whose blood paid the price for my life.

For Alma Goree and Olivia Granberry—matriarchal ancestors who held in tension love and discipline, rigor and relationship, faithfulness and freedom—I give thanks.

For Roslyn Harvey—the embodiment of the angelic who through love and sacrifice, mercy and money, grace and truth, togetherness and individuality, patience and prayer, religion and politics, playgroups and investments invited me to be whomever I wanted to be—I give thanks.

For Sorrell Harvey—who through his walk and witness in the world was a constant reminder that, "it's always about doing the right thing for the people; and if you do that, you'll be able to sleep at night." That wisdom is a lingering refrain in my pursuit of a better humanity.

For a sacred friend, brother, and contributor to this work—Willie Dwayne Francois, III—who wrestles ideas with me as we make meaning in and beyond the world, I give thanks.

For a curious, compassionate, courageous, and convicted editor—Daniel Schwartz—who invited me as a stranger to take this journey of thoughts, and turn those thoughts into sentences, and those sentences into pages, and those pages into chapters, and those chapters into this work, I give thanks.

For teaching and learning communities, teachers, administrators, students, and families in Louisville, Memphis, and New York City who courageously and mercifully compelled me to lead abolitionist(ly)—by becoming a living witness of espoused words.

For a close group of friends and family who push and support and invite me to be so enthralled in the work that they accept and cherish my often silent, reflective, and distant love, I give thanks.

And for that great cloud of ancestral witnesses, freedom conspirators, teaching abolitionists, and school leaders who continue to remind me of the necessity of struggle for such a time as this, I would have surrendered my calling, silenced my voice, and shunned my pen if not for them.

Introduction: An Ongoing Pursuit

From the moment I started school at Washington Montessori in St. Louis, Missouri, I knew there was something scientific, magical, artistic, political, peculiar, and essential about being a school leader. A regular listener in what my mother called, "grown-folx conversations," I have early memories of listening to folx discuss the work of school leaders, which was, and continues to be, misjudged, undervalued, and misinterpreted until a complaint, a criticism, or a crisis arises. But I knew what I felt, even as a kindergartener, when words escaped me for making sense of that feeling. There was a certain *je ne sais quoi*—distinctive and enthralling—about the one who made all the pieces in the school make sense. It was the charm, influence, power, erudition, magnanimity, and making-it-all-make-senseness of Black women, like Ms. Lloyd, Mrs. Claiborne, Ms. Reid, Mrs. Martha J. Christmas (a beloved ancestor whose name must ring in full) and Dr. Hardin, that instilled wonder toward the mystery of schooling. Though I never articulated a longing to become a school leader, I came to recognize that the human empathy and contrarian inclinations and intellectual curiosity and political enquiry within me, when used for the advancement of teaching and learning and care, could move schools in the direction of freedom. Then, because of those Black women aforementioned, I heard the words of "An Ante-Bellum Sermon," written in Black plantation dialect by one of the most influential poets in Black literature, Paul Laurence Dunbar, which put freedom in my soul.

> *So you see de Lawd's intention,*
> *Evah sence de worl' began,*
> *Was dat His almighty freedom*
> *Should belong to evah man*[1]

As a child, I was surrounded by Black justice-centered, freedom-loving folx who were pursuing the abolition of every angle of lived experience. It was a beautiful, bold, and brave community of Black folx who were married and single, cisgender and queer and questioning, Christians and Muslims, rich and paycheck-to-paycheck, graduate-degreed and barely graduated, parents-by-birth and parents-by-devotion, owners and renters, world-travelers and on-the-block-dwellers, poets and writers, singers and dancers, educators and preachers, politicians and executives, listeners and talkers, storytellers and story-keepers, and anything imaginable in-between. Born out of, and raised within, this tradition was my pursuit of freedom. Before her passing, I spent several moments in conversations with my paternal grandmother, Olivia, who was gracious with her time, her kitchen, her patience, and her love. I recall talking to her about growing up in Mississippi in the early 1900s, when she remarked, matter-of-factly, "Bob, I was free because I had love." As a child, freedom was a mystery to me, and even as an adult, it continues to be, because I often wonder if we ever attain it. But even in its mystery, I held that radical ethic of love from my grandmother near to my heart as the beginning of my freedom, and I have walked toward freedom every day since then—not to hoard it, but to make meaning of its mystery in order to give it to every student along the journey of my life and my calling as an educator and school leader.

I must admit—the flow of this book is unconventional, to the say the least. It is not a conventional leadership book, although there are leadership principles embedded throughout. It is not a conventional history book, although the project of abolition must begin within the context of American history. It is not biographical, although it is difficult to escape one's lived experience in abolitionist pursuits. Instead, it is an intentional vacillation between, *or* weaving together of academic prose, sermonic verse, lived encounters, airplane conversations, and personal narratives, which centers my belief about and commitment to Black storytelling as a historically relevant and abolitionist literacy tactic. Walking in the tradition of James Baldwin, Fannie Lou Hamer, Mary McLeod Bethune, Toni Morrison, Ralph Ellison, Langston Hughes, Angela Davis, and Zora Neale Hurston who intellectually yet narratively called America to task, this book attempts to call America's teaching and learning communities to task in a time when we are being challenged, as educators, to wrestle with and resolve a morass of our national identity—do we desire to be an abolitionist communally conscious nation that pursues freedom for all, or an individualistically conscious nation that reifies white supremacy? To be clear, actualizing an abolitionist approach to communal consciousness is arduous work, untidy work, risky work, dangerous work, but moral work. In this regard, we are asking a moral question—do we desire to free Black bodies, minds, and spirits, or to stiffen the fetters?

In the full view of the hypocrisy of American ideals, we—school leaders—have been thrust into a war for the soul of our teaching and learning communities, for the moral identity of our schools, and for the communal consciousness of classrooms. In a defining moment when injustice is voluble, the deafening silence of school leaders who claim to be committed to the lives of all students, namely Black students, is not only duplicitous but also disgraceful. No matter how zealously we talk about our desire to be democratic, equitable, and anti-racist in our schools, the way we utilize our voices in moments of sociocultural and sociopolitical crisis corroborates our zeal. In failing to address the white educators within one's school community who joy-fleece Black children, do your letters home matter when a Black body is murdered? When a student can be suspended and expelled in the name of zero-tolerance, what is the value of your social media posts of black boxes to stand in solidarity with Black Lives Matter? To take seriously the work of freedom and justice for Black students, teaching and learning communities depend on leaders committed to abolition, who are willing to sacrifice their power, decenter their privilege, and substantiate their voices with actions. Like silence, inaction from school leaders, in the face of structural evil, racial unrest, and global crises, is pedagogical malpractice. Period.

I grew up in a faith community where according to James 2:26, "faith without works is also dead."[2] This imprinted on me a devotion to the idea that any of our radical commitments to freedom, love, justice, and *abolition* that are absent of lived action and embodied responsibility are nothing more than democratic fantasizing. I was raised in a Black tradition in which Sundays were reserved for family meals around the kitchen table, and debates in the living room where America—its affairs, sins, and oppressions—was a regular part of discussion. In this tradition, *works* mattered. Weekly, those meals and debates were mixed with hopeful comicality as a way to make sense of our nation, with a family who believed that the United States depends on its citizens *working* our voices. A recurring theme from my iron-willed maternal grandmother, Alma Janet Goree—a Mississippi-raised, St. Louis migrated Black woman of sharecropping parents, was that anyone unwilling to act loses the ability to condemn. To maintain the right to condemn, to critique, and to demand, "we all have dues to pay." Now, decades later, that truth continues to march on: the silence of freedom-loving school leaders is complicit in affirming a prison sentence, if not a death sentence, for our Black students. And, as a freedom-loving and justice-committed Black man, I *refuse* to betray our Black students in the name of power and privilege. Therefore, abolition is the only choice.

In this day and age, abolitionism is reverberating yet again in justice-oriented spaces as a response to the American social, cultural, and political condition. The thought of abolition as a framework for approaching public education is reflexively appalling to many. That is because most of us have a misinterpreted approach to abolition, falsely assuming that the abolitionist approach is one of deconstruction, or ending a thing, as the end in itself, without making space for the idea that deconstruction is a means to an end—that end being the vision toward and actualization of a new way, a just way, a free way, a human way. Using public demonstrations, jail support networks, political education, and more, prison and police abolitionists continue to make national calls for ending punishment as a system for addressing harm, employing mental health professionals in place of armed police officers during wellness checks and crisis situations, and putting the vast funds allocated to incarceration toward the resourcing of communities that are repeatedly disrupted by the racism and classism of law enforcement. Immigration and Customs Enforcement (ICE) abolitionists demonstrate how the inhumanity of ICE's methods—mass deportations, racial profiling, warrantless searches, fabricating evidence, separating children from caregivers, and detaining people without probably cause—are directly in opposition of our nation's espoused ideals. What do these abolitionist calls teach us? The idea of abolishing a practice, a method, a tool, or an agency isn't as radical as some may think. In the same way that presidential administrations have eliminated, modified, and created government agencies in response to changing needs of society, abolition is about responding to society. With that in mind, the question should never be whether abolition is possible. Rather, the question should be how do we generate the humane, just, moral, and political will to make it happen?

At heart, the task of abolition is to imagine and actualize freedom as a humanizing experience for those who have only known enslavement, conquest, oppression, injustice, subjugation, and hegemony—the progenies of racism. By far, the most immorally void response to the proposition of abolition is as Elizabeth—a middle-aged, white principal—told me during a panel discussion: "all [public] schools aren't bad," which is the equivalent of saying that "all white folx aren't racist." While all white folx aren't explicitly racist, or act in racist ways, all white folx are partakers within and beneficiaries of the privilege of white supremacy, which functions like inescapable smog. Much the same, while all public schools aren't "bad," they all function within a student-failing, white supremacist system that participates in racial, economic, environmental, and geographical stratification. Consequentially, conserving a system because every derivative of that system isn't "bad" is the epitome of the ideology of individualism, which prizes self-reliance, self-centeredness, and personal responsibility more than cooperation, social relationships, and communal-consciousness.

When I was 11, I had the distinct privilege of conversing with Dr. Maulana Karenga, founder of the pan-African holiday, Kwanzaa, after my mother and I attended a lecture of his in St. Louis. Against the backdrop of his complicatedly personal criminal legal narrative and how it clouds the goodness of what he offered Black communities, our conversation is imprinted in memory as fundamental to my freedom pursuit. As he signed my copy of *Narrative of the Life of Frederick Douglass, an American Slave*, I asked him: "what principle of Kwanzaa speaks to you, more than all the others?" Without hesitation, he replied,

> *Ujima*, my young brother. It is *only* about our communal commitment to work and responsibility. If you have a problem, it's my problem; and if I have a problem, it's your problem. We must refuse to detach ourselves from the problems and struggles and poverties of our brothers and sisters; we must solve them together, because *together* is the freedom way.

In the car, I opened my book to see what he had written; it read, "In the struggle together." Those four words are why the poisonousness of American individualism that resides at the core of public education is perilous to the future of our republic for Black folx, because it advances the proposition that "all [public] schools aren't bad." It is individualism that cerebrally gives white folx a defense to deny their complicity in the reification of structural racism, by alleging "personal responsibility." As a Black educator, school leader, and now superintendent, I have rejected the notion that freedom and individualism can coexist within teaching, learning, and care communities; and instead, I have accepted that freedom is exclusively a consequence of communal consciousness and cooperation. For me to be free, for my family to be free, for women to be free, for brown folx to be free, for indigenous folx to be free, queer folx to be free, for trans-folx to be free, income-insecure folx to be free, for unhoused folx to be free, for rural folx to be free, for immigrants to be free, for formerly incarcerated folx to be free, for chronically ill folx to be free, for young folx to be free, for seniors to be free, for neurodivergent folx to be free, for (dis)abled bodies to be free, and for all other oppressed folx to be free, *Black folx must be free*—because freedom ain't about individualism, freedom is about community.

Pursuing the freedom of all oppressed folx, particularly Black young folx—students, has been and continues to be a journey for me. This pursuit has only deepened as the American democratic project undergoes a long-deferred racial reckoning, political reconstruction, global repositioning, and moral reformation. Now, after experiencing crisis after crisis—from the ongoing water crisis in Flint to an epidemiologic pandemic impacting the world to the increasing family separation with undocumented citizen families to the thickening blood of Black bodies killed by police—our schools are invited to pursue an abolitionist approach within our teaching and learning communities. By accepting this invitation, we must confront our deepest oppressive acts in order to imagine our communities with new possibilities and practices that lead our students, and ultimately, ourselves to freedom.

In an ongoing pursuit.

Notes

1. Braxton, Joanne M. (1922). *The Complete Poems of Paul Laurence Dunbar*. New York: Dodd, Mead & Co., 14.
2. James 2:26 (New Revised Standard Version Bible).

1

Take Refuge in How: An Abolitionist Approach to Communal Consciousness in Teaching, Learning, and Care

When she was *only* eleven years old, Pecola Breedlove is raped and impregnated by her father, and spends her life holding the tensions of her psychological and spiritual nightmare, the systemic impact of whiteness on her ideals of truth, and a faulty worldview obscured by misery, regret, and shame. But the most pernicious effect of her trauma is an unremitting pursuit to make meaning of freedom and inherent dignity within her Lorain, Ohio community, which has all but abandoned her. An incestuous rape leaves us wanting to understand why a crisis like this happens, blemishing the psyche and communal consciousness of a young girl for the rest of her life. Pushing against our longing for *why*, Toni Morrison offers us wisdom.

> There is really nothing more to say—except why.
> But since why is too difficult to handle, one must take refuge in how.[1]

Although *how* can feel like it is a poor refuge when measured against our human partiality for understanding why crises happen and why trauma occurs, it is *how* that becomes a beacon of moral light in our complex and mysterious pursuit of freedom and dignity in this nation.

Nothing reveals the moral convictions, ethical values, emotional muscle, psychological vitality, pedagogical creativity, operational wherewithal, and communal consciousness of a teaching and learning leader like how one makes meaning of, and acts in response to, a crisis. More than that, sociocultural and sociopolitical crises can abruptly expose the racial politics of a school leader. Will the school leader confront, and speak to, the crisis explicitly with the community? Will the school leader utilize the crisis as a moment to move the community toward a just and emancipated future for all students? Will the school leader take action "by any means necessary" to ensure a restorative environment in response to the traumatization of the crisis on the cognitive and emotional wellness of students? Will the school leader ensure a strategy that imagines a more equitable democracy within and beyond the classroom? Will the school leader appropriate an individualistic consciousness that leaves students without advocacy, or an inclusive-lens that positions themselves as part of the crisis?

At its core, this book deals with the intersection of school leadership, crises, abolition, and communal consciousness—each of which are expansive enough to stand in isolation of the other. It is not intended to be *the* definitive work on leading schools in times of racial crisis, nor is it an attempt to offer a technical-manual of crisis procedures, protocols, and policies for school leaders. Let's be clear. This is not a manual, but this is a reflective, inquiry-centered approach to abolitionist leadership. This is not a textbook, but this is an analysis of history as a framework for meaning-making of an abolitionist framework to form and inform our school communities in today's racially polarizing and politically jocose climate. This is not an answer, but this is an invitation to take a journey of questions to arrive at your own answer for your own school community within your own context. Taken as a whole, it is an experiential, humane treatment of how school leaders take seriously the impact and influence of intersecting and compounding crises on the living fabric of teaching and learning communities that serve disproportionately higher numbers of Black and brown students; and hence, it is how to develop and utilize an abolitionist approach to cultivating a communal consciousness.

Teaching is political. Learning is political. Schooling is political. Community is political. Leadership is political. Crisis is political. Crisis is racial. Crisis is social. Crisis is cultural. Crisis is environmental. Crisis is economic. Crisis is emotional. Crisis is moral. Crisis is spiritual. Crisis is radical. None of these things, even with our well-meaning attempts, is unbiased and impartial. Therefore, as abolitionist school leaders, we have a responsibility and a burden to interrogate every crisis that informs the landscape of our teaching and learning communities in order to expose the moral myths of American democracy that we might achieve a more perfect union. James Baldwin wrote in 1962, "It is, alas, the truth that to be an American writer today means mounting an unending attack on all that Americans believe themselves to hold sacred."[2] With that spirit, it is the truth that to be an abolitionist—an abolitionist educator and an abolitionist school leader—in America today is to pursue emancipation, by any means necessary, for all of our Black students from the systemically oppressive and subjugating ideas that public education holds sacred in the name of high expectations, grit, persistence, and success. As in Baldwin's view of the writer, it is my view of the task of school leaders to hold America accountable for its promises of *liberty and justice for all*—underscoring the all, inclusive of Black students in predominantly Black classrooms, in predominantly Black schools, in predominantly Black communities—is a moral one; and in the task before us, we must see social, cultural, and political crises as a continued confrontation with a moral mirror that forces us to see beyond the myths of good intentions and face the truths of oppressive impact.

With ever-increasing sociocultural and sociopolitical complexities plaguing the American democratic project, an increasing amount of science underscoring the impact of global warming, and the debt of racial injustice being exposed at every corner and in every institution of this nation, crisis is, and will continue to be, as much part of the fabric of our school community as teaching and family engagement. The impact of a crisis, particularly racial crises, is not limited to the heart and mind and learning within the school community, but has a ripple effect of economic burden, often resulting in food, housing, and income insecurities within families of the school community, budget cuts and layoffs impacting teachers and staff, and a loss of confidence about the moral commitment of the school and its leader, which can cause declines in morale, engagement, and in due course, enrollment.

Many crises are the result of climatic phenomena, such as unexpected weather disasters, like devastating and deadly tornadoes in Nashville, Tennessee that impact our socioenvironmental context causing trauma in displaced students and families. Others are the result of preventable sociocultural and sociopolitical phenomena, such as the still-unresolved water crisis in Flint, Michigan, or the unprecedented immigration raids by ICE in Morton, Mississippi, during which more than 680 undocumented workers were arrested on the first day of school, separating students from families. Regardless of cause and context, what connects every school leader is the ubiquitous regularity of crises, from the mundane to the epic, which always have and always will demand the imagination, and reimagination, of a *new normal* in the lives of our teaching and learning communities. Therefore, we must do the work of imagining in abolitionist ways that seek the emancipation of all students. In practice, an abolitionist leader offers teaching and learning communities an imagination of freedom before it's realized; to do otherwise is a gross negligence of our callings, titles, compensation, power, influence, and trust.

If we are going to do our due diligence in proposing an abolitionist ethic for leading schools in times of crisis, our first stop must be to frame what a "crisis" is and perhaps just as importantly, what it is not (in the context of school leadership, and in the context of this book). While we regularly absorb headlines about and carry angst engendered by a range of daily strife—from the insufferable political torture of those living under global authoritarian regimes to an NFL team absurdly stalled in determining a non-racist, non-xenophobic, non-colonial, non-imperialistic name—it would be reasonable to assume that every challenge we face within the public domain is a crisis. Our exploitation of the word itself is habitually indefinite, indiscreet, and insensitive. With its etymology in the Greek verb *krinō*, meaning to "separate" or "judge," the Greeks used the concept (classically within law, medicine, theology, and philosophy) to denote having to separate or judge (as a matter of intentional choice) between two categorical alternatives. In our time, these might include racism and anti-racism, individualism and community, teaching to assess and "teaching to transgress," food apartheid and food justice, voting rights and voting suppression, mass incarceration and trauma-responsive care. Now, in its semantic expansion, "the concept of crisis, which once had the power to pose unavoidable, harsh, and non-negotiable alternatives, has been transformed to fit the uncertainties of whatever might be favored at a given moment."[3] Intuitively, this gradual adaptation of casual deployment is at the root of our exploitation of the word.

A number of academics, management researchers, and crisis-practitioners have attempted to offer an extensive framework for measuring and categorizing events and moments into types of crises faced by leaders and organizations—along with conditions and risks associated with each type. Ian Mitroff, regarded as a leading thinker in the academic study of crisis management, proposes that there are six types of crises: economic, information, destruction of property, human resources, reputational, and violent behavior.[4] Andrew Griffin, privileging the risks at categorizations based on the crisis' emergence from within or beyond the organization, offers a four-part framework: safety and performance (internal), security and policy (external).[5] While both of these models provide valuable insights into the classical sense of crisis management and attempt to order the complex nuances of crises into easily comprehended categories, both fail to capture the inimitable culture of teaching and learning communities.

In fairness, both Mitroff and Griffin would contend that these models should not be taken too literally because crises, by nature of being crises, neglect to function in assigned categories. Accordingly, the level of complexity that exists between the "same" types of crises differs enormously by contexts. A student murdered by a known assailant is intensely different from a student murdered inadvertently by a stray bullet of violent-crossfire, which is profoundly different from a student murdered by mass shooting; the same typology of crisis, the same outcome, and the same mourning, but different in so many ways. As a result, for the sake of our analysis, there are five criteria that must be realized, each of which runs deeply through any crisis. These are as follows:

1. The situation was unexpected, unpredicted, and *unprepared for* in the quotidian reality of the community.
2. The situation has yielded high levels of uncertainty and unease within the community.
3. The situation, whether kept private or exposed in the public domain, will mark a sociocultural, sociopolitical, or socioemotional imprint on the community and/or its members, particularly its students.
4. The situation threatens to destabilize the community and its members in ways that will demand emotional, cognitive, operational, financial, and/or reputational healing.
5. The situation exposes a sociocultural, sociopolitical, socioenvironmental, and/or socioemotional injustice or oppression.

All five are critical. All five are necessary. All five are at the core of our working definition of crisis—any unexpected communally conscious situation with high levels of uncertainty and unease oppression and injustice, that, in private or in the public domain, has sociocultural, sociopolitical, and/or socioemotional impact, influence, and implication, thereby threatening to destabilize the emotional, environmental, operational, financial, or reputational well-being of a community and its members. It is perhaps verbose, but the appeal of this definition is that it manages to balance the intersection of humanity and pragmatism in ways that are accessible, applicable, and assessable.

Of course, this definition must be employed deferentially and aptly as not to exploit it as pacification for the sociocultural, sociopolitical, and socioemotional impact of the isms and phobias plaguing teaching and learning communities unremittingly. That is, America's original sin of racism is *not* the crisis; the economic, housing, criminal justice, healthcare, and educational insecurities rooted in racism *are* crises. In October 2018, I recall spending time in conversation with the Reverend Dr. Virgil Wood, a nonagenarian and civil rights icon who served as a deputy to the Reverend Dr. Martin Luther King Jr., leading the nonviolence movement work for the state of Virginia. In our conversation around crises impacting the public domain, particularly public schools in major, urban cities, he shared that it would be a coarse injustice to frame the experiences of Black (school) communities during the 1950s and 1960s in the ways we think about crises today, because life itself for so many in Black communities across this nation was a crisis. He remarked,

> Think about it like this, in the Jim Crow South, just trying to survive the plights and poverties of being Black was a crisis—a daily crisis. When didn't have mass shootings, and we certainly wouldn't have considered a protest a crisis, because we were trying to survive. Even the bombing of those beautiful four little Black girls at 16th Street [Church] wasn't a crisis. It's racism. Racism ain't a crisis. And we can't allow white supremacy to tell us that racism is a crisis as if it's an episode in America's drama. It is America—and it is American.

Crises are distinct from the isms and phobias themselves. Crises are distinct from problems. Crises are distinct from annoyances. Crises are distinct from displeasures. Crises are distinct from irritants. Crises are distinct from emergencies. Crises are distinct from disruptions. Yet there are situations (initially only thought of as any of the aforementioned) within school communities that have the capacity to escalate to the level of a crisis, and thus a school leader must always be in a state of imagination to unhesitatingly navigate the human-ambiguity and communal consciousness of a crisis at any given moment. The ubiquity of crises in our national headlines, coupled with their evolving impact on school communities and the subjectivity of how to lead during and through them, provides a catalyst to consider an alternative approach to communally conscious education. This approach would forefront the intersection of Black liberation, educational freedom, trauma-responsiveness, and radical humanity—an *abolitionist approach* that in a way involves, but extends beyond, conventional leadership practices.

Strengthening in enormity, density, regularity, and complexity, every crisis has the capacity to yield itself to us—school leaders committed to an abolitionist approach—as a vehicle for deepening our sense, understanding, and practice of communal consciousness. Crises unavoidably tear at the fabric of our school communities, placing an irreversible imprint on students, families, and staff, whether it be a global pandemic killing more than 425,000 in the United States and more than 2.15 million worldwide; a riven congressional climate where food, housing, healthcare, and reproductive justice are habitually at risk of being overturned; unrelenting mass shootings in assumedly safe spaces like churches, mosques, movie theaters, and schools; families being separated at this nation's southern border; or police murdering innocent Black, brown, and transgender citizens. These sociocultural, sociopolitical, and socioemotional situations threaten to adversely impact school communities, including students, families, teachers, and staff, but they also invite school leaders to utilize an abolitionist approach to do the work of educating, by liberating, our nation's children. Ah, an invitation.

In effect, every crisis is an invitation for school leaders to embody abolitionist principles as a way to move our school communities *from compartmentalized individualism and capitalistic-labor mills to interdependently inclusive collectivism and emancipated thought-incubators.* It is in the crucible, chaos, and confusion of crisis that our role as school leaders reaches its most critical, most discernable, and most instrumental state of being, because for Black and brown students, crisis is often a traumatizing and retraumatizing reality that demands leadership willing and able to balance healing and strategic planning, hope and operational assessments, love and accountability metrics, and restoration and communication protocols. As school leaders wrestle with all that is required in responding to and building from crisis, these situations provide a compelling backdrop in making sure that our crisis response and building are humanizing, emancipating, and deconstructionist in the spirit of abolition.

As a school-system leader and teacher who has worked with students of all races, socioeconomic statuses, and ages, from prekindergarten to doctoral students, I am more convinced than ever that *only* an abolitionist approach to leading schools will challenge and change the conditions faced by Black and brown students in this country; and that only through an abolitionist approach to communally conscious education can we construct teaching and learning communities that destabilize the systems of oppression that have facilitated the cognitive-enslavement complex in classrooms across the nation.

In our contemporary moment, abolitionism has been publicly misappropriated as sociopolitically extremist. Put the individual label of abolitionist aside for a moment, however, and think of abolition as an embodiment and a way of being. A label holds a certain amount of impermanence, whereas an embodiment, once fully realized, becomes an inescapable way of seeing, walking through, and interacting with the world. We sometimes rely on labels to find community, whereas we build and become community through embodiment, because we must become one with a shared ideal. For our work together, we must situate ourselves as abolitionists rooted in, and built upon the freedom tradition against slavery and racism dating back to the early 1800s. We must situate ourselves within a freedom tradition when Black folx, and a syndicate of well-meaning white folx, dared to imagine themselves embodying and living out the democratic ideals of the American project without the subjugation of shackles. As such, for our time together, an abolitionist is,

> a passionately human, radically moral, no less divine freedom conspirator who embodies (or is consumed by) the principles of collective community power, the transformative justice of love, the universal emancipation of all oppressed people, the dismantling of subjugating social systems, and the practice of imagining and pursuing a new world, a new way, and a new witness.

Of all these principles, it is the emancipation of all oppressed people that proffers the most daunting invitation, because for abolitionists, *all means all*—inclusive of our oppressor. Du Bois offered a liberating truth for those committed to Black and brown folx, "The degradation of [wo]men costs something both to the degraded and those who degrade."[6]

Recent pedagogical theory and teacher development have emphasized that culturally relevant teaching, cultural responsiveness, and culturally responsive-sustaining education must be embraced to be deemed equitable and anti-racist. In these discourses, the voices, experiences, and knowledge of Black and brown students are privileged as assets in teaching and learning. However, the words "relevant" and "responsive" pose an opportunity for critical deconstruction within an abolitionist approach to leading schools. Abolitionists understood that responsiveness wasn't the fullest embodiment of freedom, because abolitionist-minded, abolitionist-apologist, and abolitionist-adjacent folx (particularly white northerners) were responsive—the act of responding to a schema or stimuli. But responsiveness is not a correlated indicator of altered consciousness, wherein the mindset of the respondent is operating out of a sense of duty to the thing as an end itself and not as a means to an end. Therefore, this book calls for an abolitionist approach of communal consciousness.

An Abolitionist Reflection

Before a school leader can lead a teaching and learning community toward a communal consciousness with an abolitionist approach, they must be willing to confront their pedagogical soul. To start, identify a recent crisis within your leadership history, or that you are currently facing, and then ask yourself this series of reflective questions.

1. Based on the abovementioned framework for an abolitionist, how did my handling of the crisis create an opportunity for me to hold my community as a passionately human, radically moral, no less disciplined freedom coconspirator?
2. Based on the principles of the abolitionist definition, which do I intuitively embody? And which do I need to actively work toward embodying?
3. What school-based, district, organizational/institutional, or environmental factors—policies, practices, protocols, funding formulas, governance structure, budgeting processes—demonstrate a commitment to universal emancipation from all forms and aspects of oppression, for all students?
4. What school-based, district, organizational/institutional, or environmental factors—policies, practices, protocols, funding formulas, governance structure, budgeting

processes—contribute to the cognitive and socioemotional enslavement of students, particularly Black students?
5. What am I willing to do, disrupt, and deconstruct to hasten the day of freedom for the millions of Black and brown students in public schools across this nation?

A note for white educators—in order to embrace an abolitionist approach to leadership, it is *not* necessary to share the race, socioeconomic class, or any of the lived experiences of your students. You can be urban-reared, suburban-raised, or rural-bred; religious, spiritual, or atheist; democrat, republican, or independent; heterosexual, queer, or asexual. It does not matter. What *does* matter is that you have morally solvent concern for Black and brown students and that you want to do right by all students as to ensure that all students realize freedom from oppression, including your oppression. What *does* matter is that, in every decision, strategic plan, operational framework, and pedagogical practice, you regard the inherent dignity of all students, and as a result, seek to abolish, rather than reform, student oppression, cognitive enslavement, and/or behavioral exploitation.

An Abolitionist Approach—Nine Rhythms

1. An abolitionist approach maintains that all students are sentient (and sacred, inherently good) beings, and as a result have an inherent right—the right not to be treated as the property of an education system or a prison-industrial complex, but to only be treated with dignity and respectability.
2. An abolitionist approach intentionally integrates people and place, recognizing that the pursuit of freedom for all oppressed identities demands an understanding of the ways identities are formed by, and inform, the place in which those identities are situated. Therefore, the web of destiny that points toward freedom is not people over place, or place over people—but people and place mutually.

3. An abolitionist approach recognizes, assents, and demands that a student's right to freedom means that we must abolish, and not merely reform, institutionalized academic exploitation, since reform integrally assumes the foundation of education systems is without deficiency.
4. An abolitionist approach upholds that the freedoms of being, thinking, and discoursing are a moral baseline in producing knowledge within all classrooms, and that the radical creativity of student imagination to make sense of their freedoms by producing knowledge must be the cornerstone of teaching, learning, community, and care.
5. An abolitionist approach vehemently rejects, and seeks to abolish, all forms of human discrimination within and beyond classrooms—including racism, white supremacy, sexism, heterosexism (homophobia), patriarchy, cisgenderism (transphobia), xenophobia, colorism, nationalism, classism, ageism, ableism, colonialism, ethnocentrism, nativism, religious imperialism, and all other isms and phobias we lack cognizance of—valuing the interconnected freedom of all oppressed people in the pursuit of universal emancipation.
6. An abolitionist approach refuses the oversimplification of single-story narratives to make knowledge, make sense, and make meaning of the complex histories, voices, stories, images, emotions, and experiences within students' lives, and privileges complexity as a feature of inherent human dignity.
7. An abolitionist approach commits to healing and humanizing acts of accepting, listening, discoursing, understanding, loving, laughing, empathizing, and hoping within classrooms, not only as social-survival techniques but also as resistance mechanisms to lessen, and effectively abolish, the reach, power, size, scope, grip, and impact of cognitive and socioemotional harm inflicted by oppressive systems, structures, practices, policies, and protocols within school communities.

8. An abolitionist approach actively invites students and communities to participate in creating, embodying, and actualizing a vision for abolition and expanding a moral framework to see beyond the limits of prejudice by deepening relationships through passionate-proximity and conscious-compassion in order to understand, unlearn, and undo all forms of dominance.
9. An abolitionist approach affirms that "hope is invented everyday."[7]

Periodically, throughout your reading, return and ground yourself in these nine rhythms—listening to, reflecting on, dancing with, and making connections across your lived experiences, philosophical truths, pedagogical praxis, and abolition.

An Abolitionist Vision

The eighth rhythm calls on those of us who are committed to an abolitionist approach in our leadership to participate—with our students and communities—in creating, embodying, and actualizing a vision for abolition. I can recall my beloved mother, Roslyn, in all of her Black, saintly wisdom saying, "Don't you ever, *and I do mean ever*, demand something of others, especially people who see and trust you as their leader, that you won't do yourself—it is the epitome of hypocrisy, and I didn't raise a hypocrite." To invalidate any claims of hypocrisy, and more importantly, to not disappoint my mother, I endeavor to conceive of a vision of abolition for Black students, Black classrooms, Black schools, and Black teaching and learning communities. I use Black from this point to be inclusive of all shades of blackness and browness. Visioning demanded a question—the same question, I invite you to ask of your own community—what is, if fully actualized, the intent of abolition? Not so much the abolition of individual student lives or singular policies within schools, but the abolition of an entire schooling system that privileges assessments as indicators of value, stratifies students on nineteenth-century grading scales, and pays teacher wages comparable to the industrialization era. Not abolition as a cloak for reform, but abolition as a vision for a new way of teaching, learning, and care.

Abolition would mean an inclusive and moral division of the United States Department of Education that empowers, mobilizes, and resources its students and teachers equitably—ensuring the highest level of resources in response to the highest level of need, which would privilege urban and rural communities. Abolition would mean a plethora of historically situated, racially relevant, culturally contextual, communally conscious curricula that unerringly and authentically depicts Black brilliance, Black suffering, Black resilience, and Black participation in the nation-building of America and in culture-building of the world. Abolition would mean a federally mandated teacher-wage minimum that accounts for the time, investment, and integrity needed to ensure a cognitive, literary, mathematical, and social-emotional roadmap for students who enter into classroom communities at varying points of "readiness." Abolition would be deconstructing and eliminating body and uniform policing, behavioral surveillance, suspensions, and expulsions, and creating lasting, humane alternatives to punishment and discipline. Abolition would mean a capital-building fund where our nation's schools are regularly evaluated to ensure safe environmental conditions for learning. Abolition would mean clean water, working toilets, asbestos removal, tiled ceilings, and natural lighting. Abolition would mean nutritional wellness and healthy food options for breakfast, snack, lunch, and supper for every student and family. Abolition would mean access to school-based, preventative healthcare regardless of insurance. Abolition would mean demilitarizing school safety by eliminating guns, tasers, handcuffs, restraining devices, and all forms of militarized paraphernalia from safety officers. Abolition would mean increasing our investment to provide social worker-to-student and psychologist-to-student ratios at an equivalent ratio of teachers-to-students. Abolition would mean a willingness to deconstruct and then construct new academic proficiency metrics to account for the indigenous, inherent knowledge that students bring into the classroom without a need for scaling knowledge. Abolition would mean for white educators to show up as coconspirators, not well-meaners, allies, or accomplices, in the exhausting and exhaustive work of calling other white educators in and out on their micro-aggressions, macro-aggressions, implicit biases, explicit biases, and racism. Abolition would be restructuring pathways to teacher preparation programs as a means to widen access for Black and brown and indigenous folx with the will to do this work, but not the resources. Abolition looks like white school leaders—public, charter, and Independent, and religiously affiliated in and of predominantly Black school communities—yielding power to Black folx whom at the most essential baseline identify with the racial realities, racial nuances, racial politics, racial trauma, and racial burdens of the students being cared for. Abolition looks like local boards of education ensuring an equitable percentage of representation that aligns to the demographics of the community. Abolition would mean annual salary audits of all schools that receive public funds of even one dollar to ensure racial compensation equity for equivalent titles and responsibilities. Abolition would be a radically human, trauma-responsive paid-time off (PTO) policy for all teachers and staff. Abolition would mean restructuring and even eliminating our metrics of attendance and tardiness as indicators of family engagement. And abolition is delaying the reopening of school buildings in our most vulnerable communities after a global pandemic, reallocating the monies saved from not operating to supplement the food, health, and income insecurities of families. For any abolitionist vision, we must hold to the paraphrased, poetic wisdom of Robert Browning—that our "reach should exceed our grasp, or what's a heaven for?"[8]

Without a vision for abolition, the students in our school communities are plagued to continue enduring a white, capitalist, patriarchal imagination of people like Thomas Jefferson, who led the American empire in envisioning public schooling to stratify "the laborers and the learned." Alas, this is now your invitation to purposefully and meaningfully disrupt the Jeffersonian imagination that inherently rejects the dignities, limits the possibilities, denies the opportunities of Black students, and invites the reconstruction of an America where an equitable, abolitionist vision is realizable.

Communal Consciousness

This abolitionist vision must be rooted in the idea of communally conscious education, which this book bases in the core sociological concept of *collective consciousness*, which refers to a set of shared beliefs, ideas, attitudes, and knowledge that are connectional and, as a result, common for a social group or society. As a social apparatus that forms and informs our senses of belonging and identity, it eventually forms and informs our convictions and behaviors. Developed and propagated by French sociologist Émile Durkheim in his 1893 work, *The Division of Labor in Society*, to explain how individuals within a community are consciously bound, "What is it that holds society [or, community] together?" was the foreground inquiry that preoccupied his pursuit. Durkheim concluded, rightly for the sake of this work, that community is held together when individuals feel a sense of solidarity with each other. It is that sense of solidarity with each other that forms the basis of our ability to cultivate a communal consciousness that works collaboratively.

With Durkheim as our framing backdrop, an abolitionist approach to communally conscious education is rooted in individuals (students, families, teachers, and leaders) within a community sharing a sense of solidarity for the pursuit of universal freedom. Thus, community capacity to experience, circumnavigate, survive, and in the end transform crises that threaten to destabilize the emotional, cognitive, operational, financial, or reputational well-being of a community and its members is grounded in those community-cultivating beliefs, ideas, attitudes, and knowledge that point toward and actualize freedom. Every community, particularly every school community, has certain sociocultural, sociopolitical, socioeconomic, socioenvironmental, and socioemotional risks, issues, and problems that are distinctive to its fabric and fiber. The processes and strategies by which a community attempts to address those issues are often derivatives of the shared beliefs, ideas, attitudes, and knowledge within that community. As school leaders, then, we must cognize that communal consciousness transcends an understanding of shared solidarity and belonging, and comprises an understanding of the sociocultural, sociopolitical, socioeconomic, socioenvironmental, and socioemotional risks that function as shadows in the soul and happenings of the community. And based on the leader's proximity to the stakeholders within the community they are leading, and their embodiment of the abolitionist rhythms the level of communal consciousness varies across and within school communities.

When a school community, and its leader, is authentically communally conscious, it is fully aware of, knowledgeable about, accountable to, and guided by its sociocultural, sociopolitical, socioeconomic, socioenvironmental, and socioemotional conditions, and how those conditions subjugate the freedom of its students. Moreover, an abolitionist approach to communal consciousness demands an understanding of the histories of the people within the school community, and how those histories form and inform the identity and environment and influence of that school community within the neighborhood in which it is situated, in order to cultivate an abolitionist vision for the future that is precise. In effect, one of the threats to an abolitionist future is a generalist vision that disregards the distinguishing truths of each school community, and as a result, the distinguishing injustices and inequities that plague the fiber of that localized school community within its sociocultural, sociopolitical, socioeconomic, socioenvironmental, and socioemotional context. An abolitionist approach that cultivates a communal consciousness for leading a rural school community of Black students in the Mississippi-Delta to freedom is of the same solidarity (universal emancipation) but a different strategy as leading an urban school community of Black students in New York City to freedom. With its history of bottomlands plantations, white-dominated legislature, Black sharecropping, and vicious lynching; and its modern day de facto racial segregation, voter suppression, pervasive poverty, and agricultural-economics, the abolitionist vision for Mississippi-Delta students must address its sociocultural, sociopolitical, and socioeconomic context, which is categorically dissimilar from sociocultural, sociopolitical, and socioeconomic context of New York City—a city plagued by its own risks, situations, and conditions.

Cultivating a communal consciousness has always been a guiding pursuit of education for school communities disproportionately serving Black students. Neighborhood public schools, historically Black colleges and universities (HBCUs), and even Black boarding schools—many of which have dissolved since the 1970s—have centered the shared solidarity of Black liberation through cultivating voices, ideas, thoughts, and behaviors that usher the community toward emancipation. From 1619, when crisis took root in the American narrative of Black life with the arrival of enslaved Africans—from the Kingdom of Ndongo (currently, the Republic of Angola)—to the eastern shores in the colony of Virginia, to the crises of the 1950s and 1960s at the height of a demand for civil rights, to the crises of today with innocent Black bodies being murdered by the police state, injudiciously labeled "police brutality," the communal consciousness of Black folx has undergone a process that has demanded that we deepen our devotion to a shared sense of solidarity. It is that deepened devotion that leads to Black Lives Matter protests in more than 550 cities across the nation, calling for justice in the name of Black dignity. It is that strengthened sense of solidarity that energies thousands of essential workers—in a demand for higher (and livable) wages, healthcare benefits, paid sick leave, and the right to unionize—in more than 100 cities to organize the Strike for Black Lives and to walk away from their jobs for eight minutes and forty-six seconds, the amount of time that a Minneapolis police officer suffocated Floyd in late May 2020.

To be an abolitionist teaching and learning leader in America today is to seek and cultivate a communal consciousness in our classrooms and hallways and playgrounds and cafeterias (and even virtually) that rejects any notions of individualism that excludes all oppressed people from being free. With a communal consciousness at the foreground, the Reverend William Barber II, a minister and activist, offers us a vision for a "third reconstruction" in America. In his vision, those of us committed to abolition must "refuse to be divided by fear and continue pushing forward together,"[9] in order to do the work required in every aspect of the public domain, including our schools and classrooms, so that folx will see that "when any of us suffer, all of us suffer."[10] This communal-suffering can be witnessed in the nationwide unrest and protests, from Portland to Kansas City to Chicago to D.C., as divergent groups and diverse demographics converge in the name of justice—Black millennials, white suburban mothers, Generation Z'ers, baby boomers, seniors of all races, LGBTQIA folx, members of congress, radical leftists, and even a mini-alliance of political conservatives, like Utah senator and former presidential candidate Mitt Romney. Imagine that. This convergence is a refusal to be divided by fear, which is often impelled by a sense of individualism. This individualism has been and continues to be moral malady in our schools and classrooms fueled by an injurious use of a capitalistic ethic that promotes the ideals of teaching, learning, and, ultimately, earning being about the advancement of me, myself, and I.

In September 2014, about a month after eighteen-year-old Mike Brown was killed by white police officer Darren Wilson in Ferguson, a suburb in St. Louis, Missouri —which happens to be my hometown and where much of my family continues to live—I was in the throes of another semester of teaching, mostly Black, first-generation undergraduates. While serving as a vice president and chief operating officer at Simmons College of Kentucky in Louisville, pronounced "Loo-uh-vul" (now we've settled that!), one of the nation's historically Black colleges, I had the distinct honor of holding a lectureship in the department of religion and social sciences, which allowed me to remain proximate to the practice of teaching. That year, I was launching a new course I had developed titled, "Foundations of Human Dignity," where we explored the increasingly complex intersection of human rights philosophy, principles, instruments, and institutions, as well as an overview of current issues and debates in human rights with focus on race, gender, and sexuality specific to the United States. As you might presume, the murder of Mike Brown was ripe for discourse and debate in a class of approximately twenty Black students, ranging in ages from 18 to 35. Imprinted deeply in my memory was an exchange that ensued about the Justice Department opening a broad civil rights investigation to review whether the Ferguson Police Department had a history of racial discrimination, or misuse of force beyond the Michael Brown case. Let's be clear, as a Black man raised in the opaque racial politics of the Midwest, there wasn't much for the Justice Department to discover anew—policing in the Midwest, as it did in all of the United States, had a history of racial discrimination. I posed the following question, "What is the relationship and tension between our right to presumed innocence until proven guilty and the state's right to apprehend us on the perception of guilt?"

As a robust and thought-provoking exchange ensued between the students—many of whom wrestled with the tensions of defining innocence and guilt within a legal context—one of the students who was actively engaging when the discussion started became palpably annoyed and silent. Without shaming him, I got his attention and gave him a head nod directing him to meet me at the door. "Yo, you went from 100 to zero in

60 seconds. What's going on?" I asked. His reply wholly captures the trauma of individualism that has become the malady in so many classrooms.

> Prof, I'm just over this discussion to be honest. I can't use this when I graduate or nothing like that, so we just talking to be talking. I'm a business entrepreneurship major. For me, it's like this—if you don't want to be presumed guilty, don't do sh*t that makes you look guilty. I get that cops be out here wildin' but we gotta' do our part to make sure we ain't giving them sh*t to wild' out over. That's my take on it, but I know if I say that, they gon' start wildin' in there…you feel me?

Twenty-four seconds. It only took him twenty-four seconds to deconstruct with an individualistic consciousness why a dialogue on the tensions of defining innocence and guilt, as we explored the dreadful and unjust murder of eighteen-year-old Mike Brown—just one year younger than the student I was talking to—had nothing to do with him. Instead of seeing the racial and gender risks associated with his own identity in the larger communal pursuit of freedom for Black folx, or even conceding the racist policing of Darren Wilson, all this young Black brother could establish was that this dialogue would be disadvantageous and impractical to his *earnings* as a probable entrepreneur. While our doorway exchange was atypical in that historically Black college context, it is an exchange, a mindset, and an approach that is concealed in many teaching and learning communities of all ages, grades, and degree-pursuits across this nation.

Crises, then, can become the medium for a pedagogical and culture reckoning—and, with hope, a reconstruction—to exorcise our individual politics for the sake of a communal one. The convergence of racial protests, a global pandemic exacerbating public health concerns, an in-progress economic recession, increasing unemployment, and declining housing security demands nothing less than an abolitionist approach to communal consciousness that seeks freedom, safety, and justice for all. At the core of historical abolition, as it must be at our core today, those of us who are committed to emancipation for all have a moral obligation to resist individualistic actions and mindsets that place those within community at risk. Whether we are in pursuit of reopening physical school buildings in the midst of a global pandemic, reallocating our budgets after double-digit cuts in funding as a result of political jockeying, restructuring safety protocols and entrance procedures after a mass shooting, or giving voice to the police murder of Black bodies in broad daylight, those of us committed to an abolitionist approach must be clear with ourselves, and our communities, that how we answer in those moments will determine the future of our students, communities, and the world. In effect, will we be complicit soldiers in the name of individualism, or will we be freedom conspirators in the name of communal consciousness?

Soldiers, a word related to the medieval Latin word, *soldarius*—literally meaning those receiving pay to participate in the fight for a nation—are only in a position to execute orders in the name of those in power. A conspirator, on the other hand, seeks to plot against power in the name of the community, by calling on, for instance, the wisdom of Tubman and Douglass and Truth. School leaders who eagerly refute the guidance of health departments and epidemiologists, thus risking the safety of all within their care, are soldiers, while school leaders who heed their wisdom, aligning their actions with moral, ethical, and physical welfare, are conspirators. School leaders who deliberately fail to affirm the lives of Black folx and trans folx, formerly incarcerated folx, and income-insecure folx are soldiers, while school leaders who affirm, hold space for, and work alongside the aforementioned folx are conspirators. School communities—students, families, teachers, and staff—in crises moments get to decide: will we follow a soldier who will only execute as they are told by the powers that be, or will we follow a conspirator who will conspire *with us* to see the freedom, safety, and justice for all?

Since the signing of the Emancipation Proclamation, freedom, safety, and justice are not only political rights and cultural ideals but also educational sacraments—sacred embodiments and means of abolition for school leaders and teachers as the standard-bearers of teaching, learning, and community. Millions of young Black and brown students recognize the abolition of public schooling as we currently know and experience it as indisputable to a morally solvent democracy, as the only way forward toward a more equitable republic, and as paramount to achieving freedom, safety, and justice.

Freeing Ourselves to Give Students More

Early in the morning, about 6:10am on April 8, 2019, I woke up with first day of school jitters. No, it wasn't my first day of school, but as the new superintendent of our network, it was the first day I'd be shadowing one of our middle schoolers—Delvin, a contemplative and discursive Black eighth-grader at the time, who had considered matters of race, justice, and equity far beyond his years. During our seven-plus hours together, which started in advisory and ended in Spanish, he illuminated—knowingly and unknowingly—how our schools have failed to connect with Black and brown kids for years. By failing to make connections between knowledge and reality, by neglecting to center the identities and lived experiences of those within the classroom, by assuming that formative and summative assessments are the core indicators of learning, and by failing to invite student voice to be the loudest voice, schooling has itself become a crisis that plagued the minds of our nation's hope—the kids. As we transitioned from history to English, I asked what he was most excited about for his first year in high school.

> I want to be challenged. Take music for an example, Dr. Harvey. Instead of just learning music, I want to know the history of composers and writers, why they wrote the songs and what was happening in the world. I want to be forced to think. I want to learn more about the history of racism, and activism. Ya' know? I guess teachers don't want to talk about that stuff, because they think we're immature or too silly or can't handle it. But that's the kind of stuff I want to learn. Instead, they [teachers] are more concerned about our uniforms, and if we have the right shirt on.

It is Delvin and countless students like him who are the heartbeat of the need for an abolitionist approach to this work of teaching and learning. Lipman notes, "The overwhelming failure of schools to develop the talents and potentials of students of color is a national crisis."[11] This national crisis is exaggerated by structural metrics and data points, notwithstanding that every metric and data point has been formed and informed by implicit and explicit biases against students of color. Schools failing students and systems failing schools compound the impact of traumas on the cognitive development of Black and brown students in our most neglected communities—a crisis that demands the insurgence of school leaders as abolitionists demanding liberation for one of our nation's most vulnerable population: children. Clearly, then, as students like Delvin continue to experience crisis after crisis, their freedom and the abolition of our teaching and learning communities must be addressed with a sense of urgency like never before.

Black students in our schools and learning communities have been relegated to being pawns, a rued game of politicization. With smartphones and social media platforms shining the necessary spotlight on America's original sin—racism—Black students are experiencing what Bettina Love calls "spirit-murder"[12] by the trauma and re-trauma of being seen, experienced, taught, and assessed as an embodiment of burdens to the teaching and learning fabric of our school communities, particularly when white teachers and leaders are doing the seeing, experiencing, teaching, and assessing. And when called to tasks, many of our nation's well-meaning educators continue to construct internally pacifying, but externally damaging defenses for why it is not *their* fault, *their* teaching, *their* classroom, *their* assessments, and *their* consciousness that is contributing to the traumatization of Black and brown bodies. As a result, well-meaning, responsibility-neglecting educators become a crisis unto themselves that demands school leaders as abolitionist to arise in a demand for the liberation of our nation's youngest citizens and democratic populaces: our students.

For the last twenty years, politicians and community leaders have bellowed "education reform" as a cultural tactic to underscore the heresy of how Black and brown students have been maltreated in public schooling. Instead of an academic democracy that centers, empowers, advances, and resources Black and brown students to thrive in their communities and in the world, most have endured an academic panopticon that polices, subjugates, disciplines, and under-resources.[13] As such, education *reform* is an insufficient strategy to guarantee equity for the disinherited Black and brown students in our nation. Instead, we need education *abolition*—an unequivocal deconstruction of all that we know and hold to be true in order to create a new system of public schooling.

As an abolitionist educator who lives, works, and navigates as a Black being within a system of oppression and subjugation, it is of utmost clarity that there is no singular, linear path to abolishing education subjugation, pedagogical oppression, and systemic racist teaching and learning practices. Kellie Carter Jackson notes,

> The strategy of abolition was a long and winding road. A moral campaign required a change of the heart, conscience,

> and will. An abolitionist campaign with a political bent called for a restructuring of power and political systems. The abolition of slavery had to both stand for morality and institute real social and political change.[14]

On the long road to communally conscious education—where students experience an abolitionist approach to teaching and learning and care, guided by school leaders who situate their task, function, and burden as passionately human, radically moral, but no less divine—we must act. Our actions demand an understanding of the history of abolitionism as a movement that formed and informed much of the nineteenth century in the pursuit of freedom for Black folx within the American democratic project. As Marcus Garvey, political activist, publisher, and founder of the Universal Negro Improvement Association imparted to us, "A people without the knowledge of their past history, origin and culture is like a tree without roots."

Notes

1. Morrison, Toni. (1970). *The Bluest Eye*. New York: Vintage Books, 6.
2. Glaude, Jr. Eddie S. (2020). *Begin Again: James Baldwin's America and Its Urgent Lessons for Our Own*. New York: Crown, 6.
3. Koselleck, Reinhart & Richter, Michaela W. (2006). "Crisis." *Journal of the History of Ideas*, Vol. 67, No. 2, 399.
4. Mitroff, Ian. (2002). "From Crisis Management to Crisis Leadership." In *Business: The Ultimate Resource*. Cambridge, MA: Perseus Publishing, 293–294.
5. Griffin, Andrew. (2014). *Crisis, Issues, and Reputation Management: PR in Practice*. London: Kogan Page.
6. Delbanco, Andrew. (2012). *The Abolitionist Imagination*. Cambridge, MA: Harvard University Press, 8.
7. Glaude, 145.
8. Jones, Judy & Wilson, William. (2009). *An Incomplete Education: 3,684 Things You Should Have Learned but Probably Didn't*. New York: Random House, 193.

9. Barber, II, William J. & Wilson-Hartgrove, Jonathan. (2016). *The Third Reconstruction: How a Moral Movement is Overcoming the Politics of Division and Fear.* Boston, MA: Beacon Press, 122.
10. Barber, II, William J. & Wilson-Hartgrove, Jonathan, 125.
11. Lipman, Pauline. (1998). *Race and the Restructuring of Schools.* Albany: SUNY Press, 2.
12. Love, Bettina L. (2019). *We Want to Do More than Survive: Abolitionist Teaching and the Pursuit of Educational Freedom.* Boston, MA: Beacon Press, 38.
13. Foucault, Michel. (1975). *Discipline and Punish: The Birth of the Prison*. New York: Random House, 149.
14. Jackson, Kellie Carter. (2019). *Force and Freedom: Black Abolition and the Politics of Violence.* Philadelphia: University of Pennsylvania Press, 7.

2

A Tree with Roots: Probing American History to Situate an Abolitionist Approach to Crisis

Dr. Willie Dwayne Francois, III

En route to the north, against a backdrop of doubt, skepticism, and risk-aversion, a freedom conductor with a waving gun would exclaim, "You'll be free or die a slave!"[1] Named the Moses of American abolition, Harriet Tubman arguably risked her life for the cause of Black freedom on more occasions than most other abolitionists. Every freedom expedition Tubman undertook thrusted her life in jeopardy of capture or death—a jeopardy that defined her life from childhood.

At twelve years old, a mere sixth or seventh grader in our education system, Tubman entered a dry-goods store for supplies for her captors. While at the store, she witnessed another enslaved person, who left the fields without permission, experience the intense violence normative to the slave condition. His overseer demanded that Tubman help restrain him. Refusing to comply, Tubman propelled her body as a barricade in the doorway to allow the other enslaved person to escape. The overseer, a white man, threw a weight at the runaway man, but it landed on Tubman's head. Some historians suggest that she may have suffered from temporal lobe epilepsy as a result of the injury. The trauma of the injury caused seizures rendering her unconscious, although she maintained that she was aware of her surroundings. Nonetheless, people were unable to wake her when she suddenly lost consciousness. Reportedly, she once fell asleep beneath a wanted poster displaying her photo, a 12,000-dollar reward, and the words "Wanted Dead or Alive."[2] This only added danger to each route toward freedom. After nineteen successful freedom missions from the north into the slaveholding states, she said, "I would have freed more slaves if they only knew they were slaves." Tubman knew that a defection on the railroad by anyone jeopardized the entire freedom project—her life and the lives of the other passengers—subjecting them to capture, imprisonment, and torture. Armed with transcendent confidence, Tubman's assertive posture and hope-abundant rhetoric persuaded her passengers more than her gun. Risking her life for years, she refused to jeopardize the sacredness of her freedom mission and the lives entrusted to her by the historical moment. As a steady and radical embodiment of communal consciousness, a "leave-no-one-behind" article of emancipation, Tubman lived with and by risk-responsive solidarity. This history and message pulsate at the center of an abolitionist approach to the work of teaching, learning, and care.

Reclaiming the Black-Centeredness of Abolition

Despite the misconceived and misremembered history of abolition in America's duplicitous founding, contemporary activists—from the streets to classrooms and every sphere of influence in between—look to the abolitionism of old as a source and model for strategies, tactics, and moral authority. In the previous chapter, Dr. Harvey operationalized abolitionist

> as a passionately human, radically moral, no less divine freedom conspirator who embodies (or is consumed by)

> the principles of collective community power, the transformative justice of love, the universal emancipation of all oppressed people, the dismantling of subjugating social systems, and the practice of imagining and pursuing a new world, a new way, and a new witness.

Referring to the abolitionist movement of the antebellum period, Manisha Sinha interprets, "Abolition was a radical, interracial movement, one which addressed the entrenched problems of exploitation and disfranchisement in a liberal democracy and anticipated debates over race, labor, and empire."[3] Abolition broadened the boundaries of democracy and opened ground for new political passions. The work of abolition organically offers possibilities for the realization of democratic life in every area of community, particularly in teaching and learning spaces. Given the complicated racial politics of the American democratic project, that historical context of abolition is scarcely engaged in classrooms, congressional hearings, courtrooms, or social society more broadly, which is often the bedrock of the tension in contemporary social movements that evoke the language of abolition.

Though popular and significant academic assumptions further the narrative that free enslaved Blacks were merely the objects of white abolitionist sympathy, Sinha underscores, "Black abolitionists were integral to the broader, interracial milieu of the movement. To read them out of the abolition movement is to profoundly miss the part they played in defining traditions of American democratic radicalism."[4] We must take seriously that authentic abolitionism centers the experiential voices, comprehensive well-being, and moral leadership of impacted persons. Abolitionist luminaries like Sojourner Truth, Douglass, Tubman, William Still, Prince Hall, and Sarah Parker Redmond played critical roles in the abolition movement and the remaking of this democracy. An ancestral imagination animated by the memory of Black freedom fighters and white allies primes our passion for the possible, an invention of hope that freedom remains within reach. This imagination draws the impacted to the center and projects an equitable vision in sharp relief to the crises compounding the contemporary moment. And this ancestral imagination of abolitionism convinces us of the possibility for social changes because of the embodied realizations littered throughout history.

The stories and valiance of our abolitionist ancestry reach deep beneath our layered vocations as educators and school leaders. The vast presence of "the gone but never forgotten" freedom fighters powers our work to mobilize exoduses, within and beyond our classrooms and schools, from domination. A new exodus from whiteness, patriarchy, queer-phobias, and poverty—to catalog only a few origins of crisis—rewinds our memory to lay claim to the wisdom of yesterday, because a dehistoricized leadership praxis makes our work vulnerable to shortsighted apathy and hauntingly dishonors the risks of abolitionists as democratic exemplars. Abolitionism now, and then, offers us an ethic to remember the evilest capacity of a human community feigning commitment to life, liberty, and the pursuit of justice. As a hardly pursued tradition of activism, abolitionism uniquely functions as a way of being in the public domain that disabuses a nation of its obsession with moral superiority and the myth of innocence. Reticence to the concept involves much more of a fear of the historical reminders of the chattel regime that exposes white inhumanity than it does a sense of fantastical idealism.

Though detrimental to all Black life, slavery should be seen as a white problem—a social crisis borne out of the moral dereliction and grave inhumanity of a class of folx that exposed the empty promises of this nation. Crisis in this work, as a reminder, is

> any unexpected communally conscious situation with high levels of uncertainty and unease, oppression and injustice

> that, in private or in the public domain, has sociocultural, sociopolitical, and/or socioemotional impact, influence, and implication, thereby threatening to destabilize the emotional, environmental, operational, financial, or reputational wellbeing of a community and its members

and is detrimental to all life. The crisis of whiteness undergirding the slave regime of the United States attempted to obliterate the culture, soul, and well-being of Black bodies as constitutive to some patriotic project to build a free nation—a beacon on the hill. In plain sight, propertied white folx shelved their humanity as they accumulated wealth and built an economy to rival European allies and immediate adversaries. The slavery enterprise recruited every American institution to guarantee its longevity in the nascent republic—*every*, including teaching and learning institutions. In fact, government allied with white religion, normalized the attempted destruction of human flesh and minds, criminalizing Black literacy and learning. Consequently, as crisis, slavery destabilized the emotional, environmental, operational, financial, and reputational well-being of its survivors.

History as Living

An abolitionist approach to crisis critically acknowledges that this history is still alive. History is never past,[5] and as abolitionists situated in a living context, it is our responsibility to reach into this history and pull out lessons.

After the 1820s, a new wave of American abolitionists gained momentum in their battle to end slavery as they replaced antislavery gradualists—abolitionists sensitive to the disruption that an abrupt emancipation would cause for propertied white men. Many abolitionists fully embraced a moral obligation to eradicate the slavocracy from the fabric of the new world by emancipating all enslaved Black folx, ending racial discrimination and segregation, and even framed slavery as America's original sin.

The earliest approaches to slave abolition by middle-class whites centered around gradual termination of this system of subjugation and an espousal of Black recolonization in Africa—a return of newly liberated enslaved folx to western Africa. Against the complicated backdrop of a representative democracy further limited by chattel economics, abolitionists willingly employed myriad strategies to shift public opinion, recruit political leadership, and broaden the national possibility to deconstruct, not reform, racial inequity. The most reputed abolitionists demanded the complete obliteration of the peculiar institution, instead of petitioning to reform conditions related to the regime over time. Obliteration, not reformation.

Frederick Douglass—a complex American intellectual and an iconic radical abolitionist prior to his formal government post—purports,

> This struggle may be a moral one, or it may be a physical one, and it may be both moral and physical, but it must be a struggle. Power concedes nothing without a demand. It never did, and it never will.[6]

For Douglass and other freedom conspirators, demands for dignity and human decency require a high capacity for struggle and sacrifice. The immediatism of the mid-nineteenth century challenges us today to discard politics of gradualism and demand a restructuring of every aspect of our society and a redistribution of power. Our schools, our classrooms, and teaching and learning communities require an immediatism that has been delayed in the name of reform—the antithesis of abolition. Immediatism varies in meaning from organization to organization and community to community. But ultimately, advances of slave resistance and antislavery advocacy by free Black people and middle-class white people each reflected a call for immediate universal emancipation.

When William Lloyd Garrison redirected from his previous gradualist position and endorsement of recolonization of American Blacks to western Africa, the immediatist wing of the abolitionist movement accelerated in the 1830s.[7] The prominent circulation of *The Liberator* blew wind beneath the wings of immediatism and nearly brought the vibrato of the long-tenured commitment to gradual emancipation to a complete silence. Eric Rose purports that the Black critique of colonization "noted its racist connotations, namely the assumption that people of African descent did not belong in the United States."[8] Free Blacks and enslaved resisters challenged the question of colonization, eventually pushing Garrison and his cadre of antislavery disciples in the transatlantic community to endorse Black citizenship.

Likewise, abolitionists from the Revolutionary and Civil War eras practiced a pragmatic intersectionality in their campaigns to remake America—a call for which in our time remains desperate. The better of the second wave abolitionists diligently held the complexities of power relations and identity side by side, resisting the temptation to rank oppressions and deny hardships. Their service to humanity interpreted that lived experience occurs at multiple, fluid points of interrelatedness. In effect, it was Patricia Hill Collins' terms, "interlocking systems of oppressions." Their prioritization of dismantling slavery never distracted from an awareness of other forms of oppression and the execution of advocacy demanded to upend those evils. Garrison regularly drew connections between slavery and the exploitation of white wage laborers by "gentlemen of property." According to Sinha,

> In critiquing slavery, abolitions did not legitimize wage labor ... rather they drew a connection between the oppression of slaves and that of the wageworker. The [Rhode Island Anti-Slavery Society] argued for the enfranchisement of colored as well as white laborers.

> It points out that the proslavery position could be just as 'easily applied to white laborers as to colored ones,' exposing its undemocratic essence.[9]

An abolitionist approach to communal consciousness opened up the possibilities for thoroughgoing democracy and the realization of numerous justice passions. Slavery itself lived at the intersection of oppressions—racism, labor exploitation, patriarchy, food and healthcare insecurity, and education inequity. After all, the chattel arrangement yielded a racialized labor system, which yielded a racialized education system, confirming the destructive character of white supremacy and corroding the character of this nation as an experiment in democracy. To emancipate our education system in order to lead schools in and through crisis, the antebellum abolitionist movement offers a plethora of strategies and practices. I now turn to contextualize abolition as a history of personalized advocacy, dangerous community organization, and artistic persuasion.

Abolition and the Personal

Prior to his days as a gadfly to President Abraham Lincoln, Douglass lived two decades under the crushing, totalizing system he invested his entire adult life in abolishing. Born Frederick Augustus Washington Bailey, an enslaved Black man in Maryland, Douglass recounts how he paced himself down the cobblestone streets leading up to the railroad station in Baltimore, embarking on a death-defying trip to New York—a freedom excursion riddled with trepidation. He moved painfully cognizant of the terror of the slave's lot and the anxiety of running away. While we regularly give due attention to the maneuverings of the Underground Railroad, the act of braving the danger of escaping slavery alone was most common. David Blight contends:

> Eighty percent of these fugitives were young males in their teens and twenties who generally absconded alone. Indeed, [between 1838 and 1860] 95 percent fled alone.

> Young slave women were much less likely to run away because of their family and child-rearing responsibilities. Entire families with children did attempt flights to freedom, but such instances were rare.[10]

A part of this majority, Bailey disguised himself as a free Black sailor the day he actually escaped, an ingenious ruse in a city like Baltimore known to laud sailors during his time. Just two years before he ventured toward freedom successfully, the indiscretion of another enslaved Black man foiled his plans and led to a stint in jail. The local authorities transferred him back to his master, who leased him out as a laborer in the Baltimore shipyards. As a precaution, Bailey borrowed free papers from a Black seaman, although he hardly favored the phenotypical details listed on the document. On multiple occasions during that daylong commute from Maryland to New York, Bailey faced the prospect of punishment if someone identified him as runaway slave.

After twenty years of enslavement and two failed attempts, Bailey arrived in New York and worked to outlive and outmaneuver his experiences of racialized violence, laborious punishment, personal loss, and grotesque dehumanization. Once in New York, he changed his name from Bailey to Douglass. Douglass celebrated September 3, 1838, as his birthday—the day when his "free life began." He changed his name and his birthday in commemoration of his independence. For Douglass and three million enslaved Black people, slavery and freedom were personal. Self-definition through name creation and biographical adjustments model the personalization of emancipation and policy. Black abolitionists, like Douglass and Sojourner Truth, understood policy less as a function of government and more as a resource for identity-building. Imagine if we, as teaching and learning leaders, imagined abolition with students in our classroom as a personal agency of identity-building, as much as a function of governmental influence? For example, when we invite students to name and rename themselves beyond the names on official school records, it is a seemingly mundane, yet epic engagement in the personal agency politics of abolition.

In 1851, Truth uniquely personalized the policy of slavery and its patriarchal intersection:

> And ain't I a woman? Look at me! Look at my arm! I have ploughed and planted, and gathered into barns, and no man could head me! And ain't I a woman? I could work as much and eat as much as a man - when I could get it - and bear the lash as well! And ain't I a woman? I have borne thirteen children, and seen most all sold off to slavery, and when I cried out with my mother's grief, none but Jesus heard me! And ain't I a woman?[11]

Like all systems of tyranny, slavery was not about singular political personalities or parties. It was the law of the land enforced by courts, churches, Congress, and the commander-in-chief that shaped real lives. The capacity to make abolition personal—how it impacts kitchen tables and wallets, desks and textbooks, cafeterias and playgrounds—confronts the public with the atrocities it longs to unsee, rationalize, or further capitalize. A strength of many Black abolitionists rested in the oration and publications of their personal experiences, windows into their nightmares offered as a pathway to expand the window of the possible.

Perennially, it remains important to note how the president with which Douglass targeted his policy discussion functioned far outside the spirit of abolitionism. The romanticization of Abraham Lincoln as an antiracist, in fact, denigrates the resolve and political genius of the Black abolitionists forcing his hand on the "slave question." During a debate with incumbent Democrat Senator from Illinois in 1858, Lincoln argued:

> I will say then that I am not, nor ever have been, in favor of bringing about in any way the social and political equality of the white and black races, [applause]—that I am not nor ever have been in favor of making voters or jurors of negroes, nor of qualifying them to hold office,

> nor to intermarry with white people; and I will say in addition to this that there is a physical difference between the white and black races which I believe will forever forbid the two races living together on terms of social and political equality. And inasmuch as they cannot so live, while they do remain together there must be the position of superior and inferior, and I as much as any other man am in favor of having the superior position assigned to the white race.[12]

In 1858, three years prior to the first shots of the Civil War, our nation's bloodiest military engagement, Lincoln highlighted personal issues like the right to be employed as a public servant and marrying whomever you love. Freedom is always personal for impacted people.

Attending a public event, Elizabeth "MumBett" Freeman, a woman owned by Colonel John and Hannah Ashley of Sheffield, heard a reading of the Massachusetts State Constitution. The newly ratified constitution that overwhelmingly appealed to her innate sense of freedom read:

> All men are born free and equal, and have certain natural, essential, and unalienable rights; among which may be reckoned the right of enjoying and defending their lives and liberties; that of acquiring, possessing, and protecting property; in fine, that of seeking and obtaining their safety and happiness.[13]

Immediately, she decided to secure legal counsel to sue for her freedom on the grounds of the unconstitutionality of slavery. In her initial conversation with Attorney Theodore Sedgwick, a slaveholder with antislavery leanings,[14] Freeman opined: "I heard that paper read yesterday, that says, all men are created equal, and that every man has a right to freedom. I'm not a dumb critter; won't the law give me my freedom?"[15]

She decidedly weaponized the constitution against slavery. She made it personal.

In May 1781, Great Barrington's County Court ruled in MumBett's favor, granting her family's freedom, defined them as workers, and awarded compensation. Another enslaved African, Quock Walker, sued his abusive captor for his freedom and won. Ultimately, these decisions circulated in the chambers of the Massachusetts Supreme Judicial Court. The Supreme Court Chief Justice William Cushing argued that the state's 1780 Constitution and the stated American ideals rendered slavery unconstitutional because Massachusetts declared "all men are born free and equal—and that every subject is entitled to liberty ..."[16] As a result, the chief justice concluded that slavery was "inconsistent with our own conduct and Constitution; and there can be no such thing as perpetual servitude of a rational creature, unless his liberty is forfeited by some criminal conduct or given up by personal consent or contract."[17] Their personal narratives, their lived experiences and their human stories raised in the court of law dealt a crushing blow to the system of slavery in Massachusetts. An abolitionist approach is a personal approach.

Abolition as Organizing

Operated primarily by free northern Black people, the Underground Railroad represented one of the earliest iterations of community organizing in the United States. In fact, Fergus Bordewich refers to this systematized practice of resistance as "America's first civil rights movement." Like community organizing of our day, the Underground Railroad included coalition-building, community education, and investment in the agency of impacted people. With various moving parts, the Railroad depended on "conductors" to guide the slaves through the clandestine and hazardous route, "stationmasters" who owned the safe stations, and "stockholders"—the philanthropists funding the freedom excursions. "Much of what we call the Underground Railroad,"

Blight writes, "was actually operated clandestinely by African Americans themselves through urban vigilance committees and rescue squads that were often led by free blacks."[18] Runaway enslaved persons aggressively occupied the white imagination. The gross profiteering of "slave-catching" ignited by the passage and enforcement of the Fugitive Slave Act of 1850 impaired Underground Railroad operations in the Deep South and heightened the risk of danger for aiding fugitives.

History adorns Tubman, as demonstrated in the opening narrative of this chapter, with the reputation of being the most successful conductor. Easily imaged with a gun in one hand and the other outstretched to carry her passengers to freedom, Tubman's gumption earned her the distinction of never abandoning or failing an escapee on her arduous treks through unforgiving natural landscapes and the cunning vitriol of slavecatchers, aided by multiracial vigilance committees. Sinha clarifies, "Black abolitionists established the permanent, organizational apparatus of the abolitionist underground, the vigilance committees of the 1830s. A decade earlier African Americans in Philadelphia, Baltimore, and Boston had formed protection societies against kidnapping."[19] This organizing work required risk-responsive solidarity. William Still was a prominent Philadelphia citizen who had been born to fugitive slave parents in Burlington County, New Jersey. A close collaborator with Tubman, William Still—born in New Jersey to fugitive parents—assisted an estimated 800 enslaved Africans escape the southern evil of slavery, including his brother. Considered the father of the Underground Railroad and a consummate "stationmaster," he was one of the first recorded to have referred to Tubman as Moses. After the war, Still published a book about the Underground Railroad using his detailed records of his associates and his operations, offering the earliest comprehensive account of the clandestine system.

History notes that Tubman's ability to avoid capture during dozens of missions to the south was not enjoyed by all abolitionists involved in "running off slaves." Some sections of the country, particularly in the Deep South as the nation descended into war, treated "slave stealing" as a capital crime and an act of treason. As an accomplice to slave escapes, one most certainly stood trial and potentially faced imprisonment. In 1844, Jonathan Walker, a sea captain from Massachusetts, was arrested in Key West before the local authorities imprisoned him in the northern part of the state, miles from the Alabama state line, in Pensacola, where he stood trial.[20] Having lived in Florida for years, Walker's risk-responsive solidarity with "colored people" brought him imprisonment, a $600 fine, and a branded hand with "SS," which meant, "slave stealer." During that year in prison, abolitionist raised money to cover his fine and rebranded the meaning of the SS seared into his skin to mean "slave savior." While we should fervidly reject seeing white participation in the universal emancipation of enslaved Black folx as saviorism, we should acknowledge the multiracial organization necessary for emancipation in this nation. Like Walker and Garrison, white folx continue to disproportionately hold the positional power in our pursuits of freedom, and thus, we must demand white organizers to become supporting conspirators in Black-led abolitionist organizing. In the way that white abolitionists committed to slave "run offs" embraced risk-responsive solidarity to the point of bodily harm, reputational ruin, incarceration, and death, so must white abolitionists in our call for abolitionist teaching and learning risk power redistribution, salary equity, pedagogical adjustments, and curricula overhauls. Existential threats to one's participation in power and planning accompany the enterprise of organizing people for liberation.

Abolition as Artistic Persuasion

The role of art in movement-building and freedom advancement also finds foundations during the era of slave abolition. The arts, like the slave narratives, offered slavery a face—living, breathing bodies constantly sustaining wounds, physical and psychic, from the blunt of the slave enterprise. Abolitionist art challenged the human spirit of white people to see the human bodies of Black people. From the poetic art of Phillis Wheatly to the melodious, antiphonal sermons of Black preachers, the creative force of the imagination indicted the lie on which slavery kept its footing—the non-humanity of the enslaved. Abolitionist art served as a vent for Black artists committed to antislavery to affirm their own sense of humanness, while exposing the inhumanity of slavery. The art assaults the lie we cannot live with, and the system of slavery and all other racism cannot live without. In "On Imagination," Wheatley floods the page with wrestlings of freedom as her experiences:

> Imagination! *who can sing thy force?*
> *Or who describe the swiftness of thy course?*
> *Soaring through air to find the bright abode,*
> *Th' empyreal palace of the thund'ring God,*
> *We on thy pinions can surpass the wind,*
> *And leave the rolling universe behind:*
> *From star to star the mental optics rove,*
> *Measure the skies, and range the realms above.*
> *There in one view we grasp the mighty whole,*
> *Or with new worlds amaze th' unbounded soul.*[21]

Through inimitable eloquence, Wheatley gropes for a world unbound by the limitations of human bodies and impositions of her society. As one of the earliest literary expressions of Black communal consciousness, Wheatley uses pen and ink to pursue the emancipation of an entire people, Black folx.

At its best, abolitionist art elicits feelings of prophetic inspiration, righteous discontent, and empathetic accountability. Viral works like *Uncle Tom's Cabin* threw the nation into the moral mirror as Harriet Beecher Stowe crafted slave characters with feels and abundant humanity against the backdrop of violence, neglect, and treachery. With pens and brushes, artists employed intense descriptions of the raw brutality and sheer terrorism of plantation life. Other works explicitly centered the equality and dignity of slaves without overtly introducing the heartrending brutality of the slave situation. Elizabeth Heyrick, a Quaker abolitionist from England, painted an iconic image of a Black man standing upright accompanied by the statement, "I am a man and a brother," which expanded the statement vested in the seal of the Quaker Committee of the Society for Effecting the Abolition of the Slave Trade of a Black man kneeling with the interrogative motto, "Am I Not A Man and A Brother?"[22]

In teaching and learning communities, we must invite the use of art as part of our abolitionist approach to emancipating classrooms, content, curriculum, and conversations. Situated against ever-increasing traumas in the lives of our students and families, ever-deepening racial divides in cities across the landscape of this republic, and ever-widening political tensions between progressives and conservatives, each painting their picture of an American future, art matters. Art, in effect, becomes an imaginative invitation for students, namely our Black and brown students, to make sense and make meaning of the feelings and truths being experienced through pandemic quarantining, images and recordings of police brutality and police murder, unemployed caregivers, and decaying community conditions. As we look toward a communally conscious future of emancipation, art relishes and represents the truth of the human spirit.

Looking Backward to Look Forward

In order to achieve the comprehensive abolition of slavery—after the institution was rendered illegal and Black people were released from their chains—new institutions should have been created to incorporate Black people as foreground into every dimension of the social order, including our schools. For authentic democracy to emerge, W.E.B. Dubois argues, abolition democracy must be enacted—the abolition of institutions that advance the dominance of any one group over any other. Abolition democracy, then, the democracy that is possible if we continue resource equity for the disinherited, disposed, and disenfranchised. Freedom was never enough. The state of teaching and learning in our nation, the failure of Common Core standards, the lack of accountability in federal education legislation, and the increasing disparities in all forms of data and assessment are proof that freedom was never enough. Abolition democracy, as the highest moral iteration of what we can achieve, reaches beyond a simple dismantling of oppressive institutions and disruption of practices of domination. It requires creative, constructive institutions and new social arrangements—new classrooms, new schools, new hallways, new cafeterias, new playgrounds, new textbooks, new teaching methods, new assessments, new data points, new evaluation tools, and new staffing structures.

The abolitionist tradition, a tradition that animates the work of Black and brown folx like Ida B. Wells-Barnett, Delores Huerta, and James Baldwin, efforts to broaden democracy and expand the window of equity for all. Possessing a history of personalization, organization, and artistic persuasion—work that is both interstructural and intersectional—these features live in the postbellum exemplars of folx responsible for broadening possibilities of democracy. The work of Ida B. Wells-Barnett, Delores Huerta, and James Baldwin dramatizes the transgenerational impact of the abolitionist ancestral imagination and reminds us of the struggle to establish abolition democracy. Their courageous initiatives to document human experience, mobilize people-power, and affirm the sanctity of the human spirit manifest the risk-responsive solidarity of a communal consciousness, and challenge a new generation of freedom conspirators to ground ourselves.

The progenitor of the "Say Their Names" enterprise, Wells-Barnett used her investigative journalism to document and publish the names and narratives of lynching. In her quest to expose the horrific truth about white mob violence, she compiled stories of "the too soon gone" and practiced the personalization of abolition. In the *Red Record*, she accounts one error of justice:

> LYNCHED BECAUSE THE JURY ACQUITTED HIM The entire system of the judiciary of this country is in the hands of white people. To this add the fact of the inherent prejudice against colored people, and it will be clearly seen that a white jury is certain to find a Negro prisoner guilty if there is the least evidence to warrant such a finding. Meredith Lewis was arrested in Roseland, La., in July of last year. A white jury found him not guilty of the crime of murder wherewith he stood charged.[23]

Alongside the work of the artists, storytelling and recordkeeping like Wells-Barnett undertook humanize victims of white terror, keep alive the memory of the unprotected, give them a name, and a story beyond the swing of the rope or snap of a branch. Abolitionist work engages freedom through faces, bodies, families, and friends—the realities that constitute the authentic lives of the impacted.

Organizing at the intersection of race and labor, Delores Huerta represents a continuation of the Tubman organizing model. Huerta grandly practices organizing and building people-power through house meetings. A set of skills acquired during her tenure at Community Service Organization (CSO)—an organization committed to Latinx economic justice, Huerta invested in a sure model of relational organizing alongside Cesar Chavez. After the CSO vehemently rebuffed Chavez's and her plan to organize farm workers to end the glaring domination of Latinx farmers, they left to cofound the National Farm Workers Association in 1962. Meeting from house to house, person to person, Huerta organized a nationwide boycott of grapes, activating seventeen million people to cease purchasing grapes, which pushed the need on the first farmworker union contracts. Abolitionism performs the work of community education and mobilization at the risk of attracting a crisis of physical and reputational harm, consequences akin to Huerta's twenty-two arrests during nonviolent demonstrations with underpaid and unprotected laborers. The originator of the slogan that roused Barack Obama's 2008 presidential campaign—"*Si, se puede*" or "Yes, we can"—Huerta put her life on the line for democracy, including as a sufferer of police brutality from the San Francisco Police, who broke three of her ribs. Abolitionism then and now costs.

The artistic elements of abolitionism expose the hideous inhumanity of the threat of violence hovering over Black, brown, and other oppressed lives. In November of 1970, Baldwin responded to the image of Black activist Angela Davis, who was then a political prisoner on death row, on the cover of *Newsweek*, pictured in chains. Baldwin wrote: "We must fight for your life as though it were our own—which it is—and render impassable with our bodies the corridor to the gas chamber. For, if they take you in the morning, they will be coming for us that night."[24] Living as a democratic witness and literary prophet of communal consciousness, Baldwin refused to allow us to live out our lies. From fiction to cultural essayist, he betrayed the myth of whiteness placarded in our textbooks and training manuals. Baldwin says in his 1964 essay "The White Problem,"

> … since they had already decided that they came here to establish a free country, the only way to justify the role this chattel was playing in one's life was to say that he was not a man. For if he wasn't a man, then no crime had been committed. That lie is the basis of our present trouble … a man being oppressed by other men who did not even have the courage to admit what they were doing.[25]

The power of art disabuses us of the freedom to obscure our naked truths and cling to our illusions of innocence. Baldwin's writing unpacks the underappreciated truth of our siblinghood and the hideously emptying consequences of this lie of American exceptionalism and white superiority. He offers our students, our families, our teachers, our staff, and us as leaders the resources to grope for our humanity amidst the hatred, and challenges us to meet ourselves again for the first time. An abolitionist approach invites a continual rediscovery and reinvention, as our proximity to freedom grows closer.

Groping for Humanity

On Martin Luther King Jr. Day 2020, a piercingly frigid winter day, I organized a march of more than 300 freedom conspirators from the Mount Zion Church to the political center of Pleasantville, New Jersey—a small street accented by the city's only public library, City Hall, and the headquarters for our fire and police departments. We dedicated our march to championing the rights of students and parents, demanding the abolition of education apartheid in our state that impacts the academic outcomes, economic futures, political literacy, and life options of nonwhite students. New Jersey is home to some of the most segregated public schools in the nation. We took to the streets that January day fueled by outrage and hope—outrage over the manufactured crisis for low-wealth and nonwhite students and hope in the power vested within the people.

We cascaded down the residential streets as a multiracial, multigenerational network of resistance to the political-economic abandonment of our students and schools. Despite the inclemency of the weather, we produced a protest soundtrack for our neighbors as we chanted: "End Segregation Now!" "Defund the State. Refund the Students," and "Black Students Matter." We sunnily sang freedom songs with harmonic inflection: "Woke up this morning with my mind stayed on freedom. Woke up this morning with mind stayed on education. Work up this morning with my mind stayed on justice."

In front of city hall facing the police station, we centered the voices of Black and brown parents, students, and educators, sidelining the elected on our county's school boards, county leadership, and state assembly to just listen to us. One of the student speakers—a senior from Pleasantville High School—electrified the crowd with his experiences of exclusion and stigmatization by the school's staff. As he asserted his humanity and named his plans to attend college after two years of misdiagnosed learning capacities, impermanent housing, and discrimination from members of the administration, marchers roared with encouragement. Appallingly, one of the local school board members shouted, "Lies! Liar!" as he vented his frustrations about the school's policies that "nearly railroaded me out of the district." The school board member unbecomingly rushed to the speaker in an attempt to grab the microphone. Resolutely, the student continued to tell his story, a story that resonated with so many parents and students. The crowd booed the board member down and demanded her resignation. Her attempt to silence and oppress his experience bespeaks the daily crises of school systems, while the student's resistance to being silenced and singing with the marchers modeled abolitionism.

An abolitionist approach to crisis necessitates we pursue a Sankofa ethic—a bifocal practice of looking backward to look forward, at least, through personalization, organization, and artistic persuasion. The history of abolitionist resistance to oppression requires centering impacted persons, stamina for risk-responsive solidarity, cultivating a fierce urgency of now, and materializing an intersectional movement. The memory of abolitionists must seep into the fabric of existing and future movements for universal freedom. This ethic renews the emotional, environmental, operational, financial, and reputational well-being of disinherited teaching and learning communities. This ethic waters the roots of our movements with passionate resolve, visceral compassion, and communal consciousness as we survey human trauma—collective and compounded trauma—but show up armed with a transformative imagination. For the sake of our future, and the future of our students, oppression should only be deconstructed, never reformed.

Notes

1. Paris, Peter & Crump, Julius. (2015). *African American Theological Ethics: A Reader.* Louisville, KY: Westminster John Knox Press, 33.
2. Chancellor, Deborah. (2013). *Harriet Tubman.* New York: Bloomsbury Publishing, 78.
3. Sinha, Manisha. (2016). *The Slave's Cause: A History of Abolition.* New Haven, CT: Yale University Press, 1.
4. Sinha, 2.
5. Faulkner, William. (2013). *Requiem for a Nun.* New York: Random House.
6. Frederick Douglass quoted by Shawki, Ahmed. (2005). *Black Liberation and Socialism.* New York: Haymarket Books, 13.
7. Rose, Eric. (2010). "Immediatism." In *The Encyclopedia of African American History, Volume 1*, Leslie M. Alexander and Walter C. Rucker, Eds. Santa Barbara, CA: ABC-CLIO, LLC, 448.
8. Rose, 447.
9. Sinha, 348.
10. Blight, David W. (2004). *Passages to Freedom: The Underground Railroad in History and Memory.* Washington, DC: Smithsonian Books, 243.
11. Truth, Sojourner. (2005). *Sojourner Truth's "Ain't I A Woman": A Primary Source Investigation*, Corona Brezina, Ed. New York: Rosen Publishing Group.
12. Davis, Rodney O. & Wilson, Douglas L. (2014). *Lincoln-Douglas Debates: The Lincoln Studies Center Edition.* Champaign: University of Illinois Press, 131.
13. Barnett, Randy E. (2013). *Restoring the Lost Constitution: The Presumption of Liberty.* Princeton, NJ: Princeton University Press, 371.
14. Sinha, 70.

15. Railton, Ben. (2019). *We the People: The 500-Year Battle over Who Is American*. New York: Rowman & Littlefield, 40.
16. Railton, 42.
17. Railton, 42.
18. Blight, 234.
19. Sinha, 384.
20. Sinha, 394.
21. Wheatley, Phillis. (2010). *Poems on Various Subjects, Religious and Moral*. Phnom Penh: Keith Brooks Publishing, 30.
22. Sinha, 99.
23. Wells-Barnett, Ida B. (2014). *On Lynching*. Mineola, NY: Dover Publications, 59.
24. Parker, Jo Alyson. (1973) *Angela Davis: The Making of a Revolutionary*. Fort Myer, VA: Arlington House, 193.
25. Baldwin, James. (2010). *The Cross of Redemption: Uncollected Writings*. Ed. Randall Kenan. New York: Pantheon Books, 76.

3

Survival Is Not an Academic Skill: Radically Humanizing Trauma as a Means of Power in Navigating Crisis

Radically humanizing trauma as abolitionist school leaders compels us to reject the narrative that trauma, in any singular form, is at the heart of, and the guiding rationale for, some students' lived reality, namely Black students. Oft, well-meaning teachers and school leaders assume that any word, thought, or behavior from Black young folx that transcends the limitations of their prejudice is a word, thought, or behavior formed and informed by trauma. This corrupt attempt at justifying how we then criminalize and police Black words, thoughts, and bodies within our classrooms is part of what Eddie Glaude calls a "scaffolding of lies."[1] In effect, an abolitionist approach rejects the narrative that Black students are shaped by any linear justification of trauma, but that Black students—like students of all races, as a matter of being human—have endured, and continue to endure, compounding and integrated traumas that affect our consciousness, namely of which are the consequential crises of systemic racism. Let's be clear about one thing. Just as individuals—students, teachers, and staff—can be traumatized by crises, particularly the consequential crises of systemic racism, schools and school systems can be traumatized, too, resulting in inhumane policies, insensible classroom culture, unregulated disciplining, pedagogical monotony, hyper-testing, family disengagement, and impulsive decision-making. When intensified at the system, district, and board levels, the symptoms and consequences of dehumanizing trauma result in a structure that creates barriers to systemic and sustainable care, places burdens on the students to be their own source of healing and transformation, and stresses teachers, staff, and families to function beyond their proficiency. The consequence is that the very system—school communities—intended to teach, learn, and care for traumatized students, particularly Black traumatized students, becomes a place of trauma-induction rather than trauma-transformation.

Developmental psychologists and neuroscientists teach us that being able to multitask—like have conversation, scroll Instagram, and cook simultaneously—or control impulses, filter distractions, and make quick decisions is the result of executive function in our brains operating like an air traffic control system. Consider the mammoth responsibility of air traffic control at LaGuardia or John F. Kennedy Airports in New York City, managing the arrivals and departures of dozens of planes on multiple runways, with the aim of preventing collisions and organizing the flow of air traffic. In our brains—*all* of our brains—this air traffic control mechanism is called executive function. Now, consider the role and impact of traumas, exacerbated by crisis, in bottlenecking and obscuring the air space of our consciousness, thus increasing the risks of cognitive collisions as we attempt to make meaning of our lives, our families, our relationships, our communities, and our worlds. Next, think about every student in a classroom as an individual air traffic control tower (cognitive executive function) attempting to navigate the impact of traumas, make sense of crises, and avoid cognitive collisions while digesting new academic content and *multiply it by 24*—the average number of students in a public school classroom.[2] As a baseline, that is the amount of trauma that an abolitionist educator is navigating within their classroom; and if you *multiply that 24 by the number of classrooms in a school building*, that is a baseline for the amount of trauma an abolitionist leader has to navigate within the school community.

As educators, we must free ourselves from the assumption that we are exempt from apologizing to the (Black) students in our care whose trauma we participate in, either through our silence, our actions, or being complicit in reifying the subjugating structures and oppressive systems within our school communities without questioning *why* the structures and systems exist in the first place. Recognizing the immense suffering caused by psychological or emotional trauma, "which involves a wound and the experience of great emotional anguish by an individual,"[3] many of our students and school communities are also suffering from cultural trauma. Eyerman describes cultural trauma as "a dramatic loss of identity and meaning, a tear in the social fabric, affecting a group of people that has achieved some degree of cohesion."[4] Important to this understanding of cultural trauma is the sense that each student within the school community need not necessarily explicitly name or experience the consequence of the trauma. That is to say, cultural trauma impacts the communal consciousness of the teaching and learning community, thus demanding school leaders to do the work of diminishing the consequential adverse imprints on the collective memory of the community. In an abolitionist approach, diminishing the adverse imprint of cultural trauma as a result of crises—mass shootings, global pandemics, natural disasters, white supremacist insurrections at the Capitol, and/or racial reckonings in public services, like police departments and courthouses all across the country—demands a willingness of educators and school leaders to simply *admit* the adverse impact of the traumas on the lives of the students. Could you imagine how we could communally begin the transformation of trauma within students and school communities if we, as educators and school leaders, offer vulnerably public admittances of the impact of the crises in student lives, as well as our own lives, convey confessions of apology for our inability to have prevented the arrival of the crisis—when it could have been prevented, and then assure students of our willingness to embrace the rhythms of an abolitionist approach to conspire systemic change?

During my time as head of school in Memphis, one of the highpoints of my tenure, in part due to the generosity of a local foundation and a Board committed to leadership growth (both of which are ideologies of abolition), was traveling across the nation to study and learn from schools—traditional public and public charter—of all sizes, in all areas but all predominantly Black and brown in student demographic. While in Dallas, during one of my school visits, I found myself enthralled in a teaching and learning community aching from cultural trauma, rooted in ongoing, integrated crises. The mood was somber, classrooms lacked joy, teachers rarely greeted each other (let alone visitors), students' heads were mostly sunken as we passed in the hallways, and leadership essentially told me to go and do as I pleased. At lunch, I situated myself at a mostly full table of Black students, juniors and seniors, many of whom were on athletic teams; of all the students I had encountered that day, this particular friendship group was all smiles and jokes, in part because they asked if they could call me "J. Crew" because of my outfit. It was my typical travel uniform—a navy blue suit, white pocket-square, white Adidas (or Converse), and a white dress shirt. In Black culture, especially in Black school culture, a student joking with you is the quintessence of building rapport and relationship. I took the opening as an opportunity to probe the tenor I was experiencing, hoping it would contextualize and inform the remainder of my visit at the school. The group had a clear leader, who was full of charisma, charm, emerging *wisdom*, and theatricality—affectionately known as "B"; we met briefly when I arrived at the school, as he was charming the security staff giving him a hard time for being late—clearly a common occurrence based on the amount of laughter and banter that ensued.

I opened my inquiry *bluntly*, "So, let's talk about what I'm feeling as I go in and out of classrooms, and walk the hallways.

It's clear to me that something *heavy* seems to have infiltrated every fiber of the community."

B took lead, gloomier than he had been during the start of lunch, a mood collectively shared amongst the group as he answered. "It's been a year, Dr. Harvey." Let me admit that my heart sank when we went from "J. Crew" to "Dr. Harvey." Not because "J. Crew" was an indicator of belonging amongst this group of revered young Black folx, though it was, but because the changed moniker in referencing me indicated that we were treading grave waters, and the rhythm of our dialogue was about to absorb a new cadence, counted by the crisis and timed by trauma. He continued. "Remember Jordan Edwards, the young dude who got killed in Balch Springs?" I remembered.

> They just convicted that white officer who killed him. It took a year. A year, Dr. Harvey! Like damn. He killed that lil' boy, and it took a year to find him guilty. Lil' dude was only like 14 or 15 [years old]. Oh, and I know you've heard about that white chick—the off-duty officer—who went into that brother's apartment, Botham Jean, and killed him.

One of the girls at the table interjected,

> And she claims she didn't know it wasn't her apartment! How do you not know you're going into the wrong apartment? You could blindfold me, spin me around, and kick me, and I'd still know if I was going in the wrong apartment!

B told her she was exaggerating. He continued,

> Even if she thought he was robbing her, as soon as he told her he was unarmed and to get out, she could have handled it differently. It just feels like they can get away with anything. You know what I mean?

Not wanting time to assume, but knowing clearly what he meant, I inquired anyway, "Who can get away with anything?"

> White people. Well, not all white people. White cops. Plus, it feels like the civil rights movement all over again, because all over Dallas you see 'Make America Great Again' signs and confederate flags like the KKK has returned or something. And to make it all worse, some of the dudes we grew up were killed recently, not by the cops, or anything like that, but it was dumb stuff, like fighting over chicks.

A different voice emerged—a quiet and reflective soul, who went by Lady.

> Earlier this year, I think it was in February, a freshman who was only 14 [years old]—not at our school—was killed in a drive-by. She was so pretty, and seeing her face all over the news was just sad. Can you believe that? A 14 year old killed in a drive-by? What could she have done that deserved her to be taken? My little sister is 14, and I can't imagine her being killed. I just feel for her family because I know I wouldn't be normal if it happened to my little sister.

She went on to explain that the northwest part of the city had experienced unprecedented hazardous gas leaks, causing the death of a twelve-year old and displacing hundreds of families in a city plagued by affordable-housing insecurity. A silence fell over the table as we all inwardly *contemplated* the severity of what had just been shared. Breaking the silence, I scurried to humanize the intensity of the moment.

> I'm sorry. I'm sorry that you are carrying the burdens of racism, death, and misery in tension with years of your

> life that should be euphoric and hopeful. What can I do to support you in making sense of it all? Do you want me to see if I can get you all out of next period for us to keep talking?

With the soul of Ralph from *Lord of the Flies*, B replied,

> That would be dope. It's more than what the principal, or the so-called dean, and the other administrators have done around here. They act like none of it exists. They didn't even say anything about Botham Jean until we pressured them too; and last year, they were silent about the little boy who was killed. I guess it has to be one of us for them to finally say something, or one of their own kids. I mean, can we have a protest, an assembly, a sit-in, a town hall, an email, a letter in our backpacks like when we were little kids, a call home, a moment of silence, anything? Like damn! Sorry, Dr. Harvey—I didn't mean to curse. It's just so frustrating!

I replied, "Don't apologize, I'm listening."

> Even after we pressured them to say something about Botham Jean, they had the nerve to say we'd have time in all of our English classes to 'process our community's grief through writing' [as he made air-quotes]. You can't turn this kind of [stuff] into a writing lesson, but that's exactly what they do when anything crazy happens in the city. 'We're going to write about it in a reflection journal,' or 'for our Do-Now, we're going to watch a clip from CNN.' Watch the news? Are they serious? Watch the news! I don't watch the news. You know why? Because, we live the news. We are the news. This ain't a English lesson. This ain't a class discussion of *To Kill a Mockingbird* [everyone at the table collectively chuckled, including B,

> who immediately returned to the gravity of his monologue]. This is my life. This is *our* life. We don't want a writing prompt. We want a conversation. We want it to make sense. We want to know what we can do. We want to know what *they* [the school leaders] will do. So, yes, we'd love to keep talking with you … if they let you.

It is here that the uncanny and chilling words of Audre Lorde—words from a Black lesbian feminist denoting a categorical imperative—resound loudly as a demand to radically humanize the trauma of our students as a means of power and survival in navigating crisis. On October 29, 1979 at the "The Personal and the Political" Panel, which Lorde later wrote and published, she wrote:

> … those of us who have been forged in the crucibles of difference—those of us who are poor, who are lesbians, who are Black, who are older—know that survival is not an academic skill. It is learning how to take our differences and make them strengths.[5]

Abolitionist school leaders refuse the notion that surviving trauma must be a skill, a curriculum, and a period in the schedule. In communally conscious schools, trauma—when radically humanized—is a justice pursuit for schools and school systems to imagine, and then create ways that privilege prevention, intervention, and transformation. Our pursuit compels us to approach trauma, not as experiences to merely be responded to, but as a medium for students to transform pains, plights, predicaments, and poverties into means of power in the teaching and learning process. In a communal consciousness, this obliges school leaders to lead teachers in a process of creating "new ways of thinking, seeing, feeling, speaking, and experiencing" trauma *alongside* our students, which will demand "collective resistance and revolution at the scene of the 'crime' itself" (Guenther, 61). This collective, or communal, resistance and revolution at the site of the "crime" itself begins by decriminalizing the consequences of trauma, and eliminating punitive measures—suspensions and expulsions—while creating meaningful forms of systemic prevention, intervention, and transformation. Such resistance, as a response to navigating the impact and influence of crisis in students, schools, and systems, involves abolitionist leaders and educators unmasking and *expanding* our understanding of trauma, *emancipating* our language, *embodying* the centering of relationships, and *echoing* the resilience of hope.

Expand Our Understanding of Trauma

What, to the student, is trauma? What, to the classroom, is trauma? What, to the school leader, is trauma? What, to the community, is trauma?

In this age of trauma-responsive pedagogy and trauma-responsive classrooms, we all—educators and school leaders of all races, in all communities, and in all contexts—use the word trauma in everyday language to describe any highly stressful event or situation and its impact on the thinking and living of the individual who experienced it. According to classical thought amongst mental health experts and psychologists, the key to understanding psychological trauma is that it specifically refers to when a "traumatic event or crisis overwhelms or threatens to overwhelm a person's ability to cope."[6] That framework is intentionally broad because there are two intersectional components of any traumatic experience—the objective and the subjective.

> It is the subjective experience of the objective events that constitutes the trauma … the more you believe you are endangered, the more traumatized you will be. Psychologically, the bottom line of trauma is overwhelming emotion and a feeling of utter helplessness. There may or may not be bodily injury, but psychological trauma is

> coupled with physiological upheaval that plays a leading role in the long-range effects.[7]

In effect, trauma is formed and informed by the experience of the survivors, which is why and how two individuals can experience the same experience, situation, or event, then have varying emotional, cognitive, and physical responses because of the lived experience, mediated by all of our identify factors.

When Donald Trump was named the 45th president-elect of the United States on Tuesday, November 8, 2016, Black and brown folx experienced that event with varying emotional, cognitive, and physical responses. That following day, on Wednesday, November 9, I recall a handful of teachers utilizing paid-time off (PTO), each taking a "mental health day" over the news of his election. For those teachers, that event represented traumatic stress, which adversely had an impact on their ability to teach. As an aspiring abolitionist, I completely comprehended their emotional and cognitive response to his election because it included, either in reality or in perception, many of the indicators of traumatic stress—"abuse of power, betrayal of trust, entrapment, helplessness, pain, grief, confusion, and/or loss."[8] While some classical-thought mental health experts would suggest that our individual reactions to a presidential election neglect to meet the trauma criteria of overwhelming, or threatening to overwhelm, our ability to cope, the word is increasingly used to describe an increasingly wide number of situations and events. A growing number of psychologists, psychotherapists, mental health experts, and cultural leaders are expanding our understanding and use of the word by leaning into the *subjectivity* indicator of traumatic stress.

As abolitionists—committed to the *universal emancipation of all oppressed people*—the first task of our transformation of trauma into a means of power as students, particularly Black students, navigate crises is to embrace a more expansive (and universal) understanding of trauma. Just as our definition of crisis requires us to make space for the sociocultural, sociopolitical, and/or socioemotional impact of the unexpected and unplanned, oppressive and unjust, we must extend our definitions and discourses about trauma beyond the individual. Above, we talked our cultural trauma as those events and situations that tear at our social fabric and affect a group's level of cohesion, which transcends the individual trauma. Beyond the individual socioemotional and sociocultural dimensions, how could our conversations and ultimately our pedagogical and leadership practice revolutionize if we expanded trauma to include the socioenvironmental, sociopolitical, and socioeconomic?

Since the killing of Trayvon Martin on February 26, 2012, the intersection of sociocultural and socioemotional traumas has collided in sociopolitical trauma across the nation, exposing the latent hypocrisy around race and racism in the United States. The resultant traumas thus forced school communities to address—or not address—the trauma of racism in classrooms of all ages. As we have had to learn and call the names of Trayvon Martin, Michael Brown, Sandra Bland, Breonna Taylor, Ahmaud Arbery, George Floyd, Elijah McClain, Atatiana Jefferson, Aura Rosser, Stephon Clark, Botham Jean, Philando Castille, Tamir Rice, Alton Sterling, Michelle Cusseaux, Freddie Gray, Janisha Fonville, Eric Garner, Akai Gurley, Gabriella Nevarez, Tanisha Anderson, Marvin Booker, and countless others, Black students have had to experience the traumatizing and retraumatizing that comes along with each news headline that accentuates police abuse of power, betrayal of trust in community protection, and the confusion, pain, grief, and loss of Black bodies being murdered. But oft neglected in our professional development sessions and leadership meetings is meaningful thought of what trauma means for Black students—a generation stained by blood shed at the hands of white-supremacist power, legalized slavery framed as mass incarceration, mass shootings in communal and sacred spaces, and now a global pandemic that has upended any sense of human normalcy in classrooms and hallways. As abolitionist school leaders, or aspiring abolitionists, not only is it morally insolvent to limit our understandings of trauma, but it is also pedagogically negligent. Thus, the question echoes as we think about what we can do, as school leaders, within our own communities to ask and answer within ourselves, and amongst those we lead: *what is our understanding of trauma?*

In just about any trauma-responsive and pedagogy book you see on the shelves of well-meaning educators and school leaders, the question of trauma, and school-based strategies for response, are framed as individual and psychological ones. Contrary to this hyper-utilized singular framing, trauma for Black students is not able to be framed, or responded to in a singular, linear equation, nor is it solely an indictment on individual upbringing and family engagement (though individual upbringing and family engagement are worthy indicators for unpacking the roots of trauma). Trauma, then, in a Black student context recognizes the intersection of socioemotional, sociocultural, sociopolitical, socioenvironmental, and socioeconomic indicators. Thus, trauma in its most expansive form (to and for a Black student) must be framed as any combination of intersecting events or crises that overwhelms, or threatens to overwhelm, a student's ability to navigate the school community because of an abuse of power, betrayal of trust, entrapment, helplessness, pain, grief, confusion, and/or loss. That means that anyone with an abolitionist approach to radically humanizing trauma must be cognizant that students of all races and economic classes, particularly in underinvested communities, are frequently experiencing the intersection of housing-destabilizing, healthcare-lacking, income-threatening, parks-decaying, hyper-violent policing, redlining, no-child-left-behind'ing, every-student-succeeding, standardized-testing, third-grade-reading-scores-prison-constructing, building-neglecting, look-straight-in-front-of-you-hands-down'ing, teacher-underpaying, community-underfunding, dignity-defeating, dream-deferring, and voice-deafening traumas. By embracing this expansive view of trauma as intersectional, we mutually embrace that the task of abolitionist approaches to humanizing trauma is not *reforming* the sources of trauma. Instead, the task of abolitionist approaches to humanizing trauma is about atoning for the structural sins of the systems themselves—zero-tolerance policies, prison-modeled behavioral codes, unmerciful uniform demands, and white-supremacist culture teaching approaches—by abolishing the systems altogether, and partnering communally with students, families, and teachers toward constructing a new world, a new community, a new school, a new classroom, and new systems that eliminate the sources of trauma.

As an abolitionist school leader, cultivating an expansive view of trauma is not just about radically humanizing interpersonal awareness; it is also about radically humanizing accountability. When we maintain, and therefore lead, with narrowed views on what does and does not meet the criteria of trauma, we leniently allow teachers and staff to criminalize and discipline select behaviors that are beyond our individual rubric. In effect, we inadvertently drift into creating two intersectional components of any trauma response—the radically human and the subjective; and the hazard of subjective responses to trauma, by way of subjective codification of trauma, is that it places an added burden on the student (as the source of the trauma itself) to validate their coveting for radical humanity. Additionally, it places an added burden on educators of color, who become the saintly incarnations of radical humanity for the entire community. To be very clear, narrowed views of what constitutes trauma create a context for the traumatic consequences of white supremacy culture—and its many enigmas—to be healed by Black teachers, counselors, social workers, professors, academic advisors, principals, and superintendents who themselves are navigating the traumatic consequences of racist systems, practices, policies, and protocols. Thus, an abolitionist approach is to ensure that all educators and school leaders within a teaching and learning community have a shared expansive view of trauma as not to put the demand on Black folx within the community to do all of the heavy lifting in pursuit of our own radical humanity. After years of radically humanizing the trauma of hundreds and thousands of Black students in school communities, particularly in school communities largely staffed by well-meaning white educators, no wonder many Black educators in academic spaces view responding to the consequences of intersectional traumas as being beyond the scope of their role. Furthermore, given that the consequences of intersectional traumas are often invisible, or even undetected, white educators can easily misperceive students' authenticities—in their responses to questions, thoughts about the world or the school interactions with adults and students, and intentions with particular behaviors—as offensive, insolent, uncooperative, or non-participatory when, in fact, there is more happening underneath. In their frustration, white educators may find themselves reacting to, and engaging with students in ways that compound the consequences of intersectional traumas, thus requiring Black educators to work at a deficit to not only radically humanize the initial traumas but also the compounded trauma of white misperception.

"How ya' doing handsome?" a stunningly dressed, white-haired Black woman, Yvette, spoke as we buckled in for a sunny Friday afternoon flight from Atlanta to Memphis. I understand that she was a grandmother, because she took a call before we departed where she ended by saying, "Mama can't wait to see you!" Mama is a common colloquialism for grandmother in Black communities.

"I'm doing well, and how are you?"

With a glowing smile, teeth sublimely ready for a Crest commercial, she replied, "I'm doing just fine. Headed to see my grands in Memphis. What do you do that has you in a suit early this morning?"

We both laughed, and I replied, "I'm in education." It was, and continues to be, my typical in-flight answer, ordinarily as a way to situate the questions; if they probe, it is highly likely that they, too, are an educator or interested in education—even if superficially. If they accept that answer as a definitive response, it is *often,* but not always, because there was sparse interest in the answer at the outset.

She was interested. "What *exactly* do you do in education?" she asked with the gentlest smirk, which made it clear that she wanted details.

I chuckled, and then obliged the exchange.

> I serve as Head of School for an independent charter school in Memphis. Before that, I served at a historically Black college in Louisville, Kentucky in dual capacities—chief operating officer/vice president and lecturer in religion and social sciences. And before that, I worked in a variety of Independent day and board schools in New England, initially as a teacher, then in administration.

She noticed that I used the word "serve" for my roles in Memphis and Louisville, and "work" in reference to the Independent schools; we both agreed that there was much unpacking needed in differentiating those word choices by community and geography, and our fifty-minute flight did not afford enough time to unpack it. I returned the question, "May I ask what you do?"

She gladly replied, "For the next couple of months, I'm an English teacher in Atlanta. DeKalb County, if you know the city like that. But I'll be retiring at the end of the year, and thank God."

Using the white-hair and "handsome" as context clues, it was evident that she was at least my mother's age, but I had to know how long she had been an educator, so I inquired. She smiled, leaned closely, and said, "37 years. Before teaching, I tried being a writer, and then I was a legal secretary for a Black attorney in Atlanta. But teaching found me, and I welcomed the discovery."

Then, I wanted to know, "Why retirement now? 40 years is in view."

She paused, shook her head, and sighed a deep breath before replying.

> If I was talking to my one of my colleagues, I'd say that I had given all that I had to give, and now it's time for me to lower the budget by letting them replace me with someone younger. But I'd be lying, child. [We laughed.] To be honest, I gotta' get out now because I'm tired of being a teacher, and a curriculum writer, and a counselor, and a fight-breaker, and a mediator, and a court advocate, and a health advocate, and a diversity specialist, and a contract negotiator, and any other role you could imagine. At a different school with a different principal, I could probably make it to 40 years; but where I am now, no sir, no sir—can't do it! And you know what, it's not even the kids! They aren't the problem, at all. It's the teachers, and our leadership. Every time a child of color does something that 'frightens' or 'worries' or 'confuses' one of these white women that I work with, you know where they send them? To me! I could be in the middle of a lesson … a good lesson too, like when I teach *The Bluest Eye* … and here comes a 6-foot, 200-pound child pouting with their eyes telling me how they were put out by a white teacher and told to go to the office, but they rather just sit in my room. So I'll ask them, 'What happened?' And do you know it'll be simple stuff like the teacher told them to move to another seat, but they were charging their phone at the outlet by the window and didn't want to leave it, and when they bucked, they were put out; or they were eating a bag of chips, and the teacher told them to throw it away but they child didn't like the lunch so they were eating the chips instead. Instead of the teacher, mostly the white women, taking 20 seconds to figure out why asking him to move was so upsetting or why throwing the chips away was so

> frustrating, they just put them out and send them to me. Did you see how easy that is, 'Why are you upset by what I asked you to do?' That's not even 20 seconds; it's more like 5 seconds! I've told my principal that all of us, me included, need training on how to just be human with children and all of the stuff [trauma] they bring to school with them, like we try to be with our own children. But all he says is, 'You have the magic touch!' Well, this magician is about to disappear because I refuse to do white women's work for them—and that's what I've been doing for 37 years. And let's not even talk about the white male teachers who straddle between coach, warden, overseer, and wannabe-father to the Black boys. Again, it's not the kids; it's the grown folx!

Now, after months of a global pandemic, years of racial reckoning, and decades of subjectively determining how we codify traumas and our varying responses to those traumas in classrooms across the nation, it is clearer than ever that Black students, and Black educators, are disproportionately impacted by the ways in which our school communities and school systems radically *dehumanize* trauma, particularly when that trauma has been shaped by crisis. Any indisposition to maintain a narrowed view, and limited criteria, about traumas impacting the lived experiences of our students will continue to provoke a criminalizing and disciplining approach, which is inconsistent to an abolitionist approach of communal consciousness. If we can expand our understanding of trauma, and how intersectional traumas threaten to unravel the fabric of our students, our classrooms, our schools, and our communities, we will position ourselves to ask and answer the questions: what, to the student … what, to the classroom … what, to the school leader … and what, to the community, is trauma? Our clarion call will be *anything*—and I do mean anything—that overwhelms, or threatens to overwhelm, any student's ability to navigate the classroom, the school, or the community because of an abuse of power, betrayal of trust, entrapment, helplessness, pain, grief, confusion, and/or loss.

Emancipate Our Language

In society, in communities, in families, in friendships, in relationship, and most crucially—in classrooms—words matter. As abolitionists in pursuit of communal consciousness, our words become seeds of subjugation or follicles of freedom within our classroom communities. When many of us were children, particularly after an instance of name-calling, we were reminded of Alexander William Kinglake's rhyme:

Sticks and stones may break my bones,
But words will never hurt me.

What was an attempt to increase our resiliency to verbal hostility, by inviting us to take on the assumption that words are powerless, was in fact one of the earliest dishonesties of life. Words hurt, because words matter—inflicting damage in our hearts, impressing suffering in our souls, and imprinting harm on our brains. And none of us, particularly oppressed people in this nation, are insusceptible from the emotionally devastating, cognitively impacting effect of words. Oppressed people have been coerced to navigate the intentionally destructive, calculatedly offensive, and purposefully derisive use of words by folx in power, words that we can designate, on account of the 1942 Chaplinsky v. New Hampshire decision, as "fighting words."[9] The court ruled that the First Amendment does not protect fighting words—words that not only humiliate but also seek to subordinate a person on the basis of race, ethnicity, gender, sexuality, economic status, and other identity markers—because said words have an explicit propensity to ignite acts of violence. Employing the court's theory, educators and school leaders must be cognizant of not only fighting words but also traumatizing words—words that overwhelm, or threaten to overwhelm, a student's ability to navigate a community by causing humiliation, helplessness, pain, grief, confusion, and/or loss.

One might be tempted to read this, and contend that this approach is hypersensitive because students need to develop "tough skin," a refrain often uttered by educators and school leaders who privilege a capacity of free speech, unchecked tone, unobstructed intention, and unapologetic impact as a warrant to loosely use language. Instead, educators and school leaders should read this approach as a critique of positional power politics—amplified by racial and gender oppression—thus holding us accountable for intentionally using language as not to traumatize students who are commonly, but not universally, structurally defenseless in our teaching and learning communities.[10] Thus, our language must be emancipated because of what it does "to the addressee, how it assigns him or her a place in the social symbolic structure, but also by the way it forces the address to recognize the speaker's authority."[11] This is why, right from the start, I want to be clear that our concern is not exploring whether or not words matter, nor whether language has power or not. Our concern emphatically underscores that words matter, and language has power, so as abolitionists, we have a responsibility and burden to emancipate our language from being sources of trauma, and a reification of positional power politics in our school communities. An abolitionist approach contends that while words matter in their capacity to traumatize, words equivalently matter, for educators and school leaders, in their capacity to heal and to reconstruct, when we choose our words with intentionality. How often have you stood in front of a school community, teachers, students, and families using words without intention, reinforcing power and privilege? How often have you said something, and within a matter of moments from those words exiting your mouth, needed nothing more than to recant every single word? How often have you had your own words repeated, copied and pasted, or even replayed, forcing you to reconcile the damaging impact you affected? As a school leader, how often have you been in complicit in sanctioning—through silence—white educators to communicate to students, colleagues, and families using language without intention, positioning themselves as the centering power of rhetoric, neglecting to regulate the use of "fighting words" and traumatizing words?

As part of a teaching residency listening and learning tour, I found myself in Boston—a city I hadn't visited since graduating Harvard—on a cold, sunny Wednesday, twenty-four days before Ahmaud Arbery was killed while jogging in Glynn County, Georgia, and forty-three days before our network of schools closed our buildings in response to the COVID-19 global pandemic. I was there with a group of colleagues—our director of talent, a Black man, and the managing director of our teaching residency, a white woman—visiting a neighborhood-based charter school full of more than 300 Black and brown elementary students, and a throng of white, well-meaning educators, and a scattering of Black and brown educators, mostly residents. After a full day of observations and small-group sessions, we were invited to attend an afternoon staff meeting and professional development session. It started as it would in essentially any school around the nation—snacks being distributed, kids moving to-and-fro trying to figure out where to go, teachers chatting in grade-teams, a review of the day's agenda, a round of glows about a lesson that was presented, feedback on how the week was progressing, and a batch of announcements from the leadership team. Then, it was turned over to the teachers for announcements, and that's when a white, well-meaning teacher stands in front of us with an abundance of anxious energy adorned in all black—shirt, pants, and shoes—as if she was in mourning. She begins her remarks, "So, let me start by saying I'm so nervous because this is really exciting for me because I am so honored to be the chair of Black Lives Matters Week."

I immediately made eyes with our director of talent, our teaching residency-managing director, and the only lead teacher of color at the school, and we all grin while dropping our heads because we knew where it was going.

She continued with glee,

> Now, I need your help to make this a success. We need you to invite really successful Black people that you know to talk to our students. They [the really successful Black people] don't have to be President Obama or Beyoncé or anything like that; they can be anybody, an accountant you know, or a doctor, or a neighbor. We just want these students to see really good, really successful Black people. There has been so much progress in America for Black people and they need to see it. Oh! And I really, really have to thank my committee for all of their hard work. If you can think of anything else we can be doing to make this week special for them, please let me know.

Multiplying the problematic moment, the overwhelming majority of her colleagues, including school leadership, looked on with smiles and nodding heads as nonverbal cues of affirmation. All I could think to myself was, here we go again—another white, well-meaning educator using problematic, and oppression-adjacent language while being entranced by the romanticisms of talking about Black folx, Black culture, and Black progress in America. Little did I know that only twenty-four days later, her words—"they" and "these" and "them" referencing Black and brown students—would ring vociferously as a public reckoning on racism erupted in streets across the nation with protests underscoring the dignity of Black folx and inviting the reconstruction of a America where an equitable democracy would allow us to have our identity validated beyond the use of pronouns. I couldn't have predicted that in a pedagogical era where culturally relevant pedagogy books—which I contend is a more palatable derivative of "culturally competent"; remember that?—are on bookshelves, in tote bags, and on professional development scopes and sequences as schools rummage for ways to talk about America's original sin of racism, that white, well-meaning educators were still conflating cultural relevance with individual progress. It confounded me to hear a white educator use public rhetoric in declaring, "They don't have to be President Obama or Beyoncé or anything like that; they can be anybody …" as if she was explaining her fish order at the seafood counter. Words matter. Language matters. Rhetoric matters. Paralleling the sociocultural and sociopolitical progress of Black folx to the global celebrity of entertainers and athletes, or the election of Barack Obama, without acknowledging the complicated, systematic racist sociopolitics of public life for all Black folx, including the celebrities and notable personalities, is negligent rhetoric.

Against the complicated backdrop of a nation plagued by "alternative facts" and political rhetoric more oppressive than Bull Connor, white educators and school leaders have a responsibility and burden of ensuring language and words that respect the inherent dignity and identity and lived experiences of Black students within the community. The question, then, is how can white educators—and some Black ones, too—emancipate their language? One of the ways, seemingly straightforward and uncomplicated, is to abolish the use of pronouns with exclusionary, oppressive implications—they, them, these, and those—without first giving dignity to the collective group of folx we are addressing, discoursing about, or discoursing with. I am realistic enough to know that educators, as most English-speaking citizens of this country, use pronouns with as much thought as people give to using doorknobs. But, when well-meaning, good-intentioned educators, particularly white educators, casually use "them" and "they" pronouns, it creates a rigid dichotomy between themselves and the students within their care, reinforcing a subjugating power-politics that is endemic to classrooms. While we all bear this responsibility to emancipate our language, our words, and our rhetoric as part of the pathway to emancipating our mindsets, white teachers and educators have an added burden of emancipating themselves of any word, or phrase, or rhetoric that intentionally or unintentionally reinforces a Jim Crow dynamic of dichotomies—us and them. Communally conscious educators use classroom discourse of all forms—from the mundane to the epic, from threshold greetings to cold calls, from turn and talks to Socratic method—to abolish oppressive language, which is unfortunately such an embedded aspect of routine discourse in schools and classrooms that it can be difficult for some educators, and school leaders, to even notice. Thus, from the mundane—the unintentionally oppressive uses of "they" and "them" pronouns—to the substantial—our use of words that degrade the inherently dignity of a human—an abolitionist approach to radically humanizing our classrooms as a transformation of trauma is to reject rhetorical oppression that reinforces a privileged, power-centered view of the world. When educators, even the ones we honor and love and respect within our school communities, use oppressive and subjugating language in any and all forms, it not only harms the individual, classroom, or the community but also *elongates* a linguistic history of subjugation and oppression that has been inherent to the Black experience in America and its institutions, particularly in public education.

Are pronouns for pronouns-sake the issue? Of course not. But what seems clear enough is that as we advance our claims of justice, equity, and anti-racism in hope to radically humanize, and effectively abolish, student experiences with trauma, it has become impossible, however mundanely they are in our rhetoric, to continue ignoring the damaging implications of pronouns as default indicators for group identities, particularly for group identities for folx who have an oppressed history, which is just about every non-white, non-European group in this nation. Every struggle of an oppressed people, particularly Black people, has an integrated history of overt rhetorical discrimination and verbal violence, which *elevates* the significance of taking our words seriously. By using, permitting, or ignoring language—with ignoring being the most common approach as not to offend those who use or permit oppressive rhetoric—school leaders are adding to that collective experience. In this sense, racial crises provide school leaders with an opportunity to interrogate, within themselves and within their communities, the othering happening nonchalantly and formally in school leadership and grade-team meetings, data-dives and professional development, and even in sports competitions and school celebrations through language, words, and rhetoric. As Dr. Wizdom Powell from University of Connecticut, Health Disparities Institute notes in conversation with Andrew Grant-Thomas on the othering of Black folx:

> … to be othered is to be denied the fullness of one's humanity. It's about reminding people, either by the barriers we put up in social spaces or the barriers to opportunities to advance our well-being, about saying through words or actions, that "you're not one of us."[12]

As education, our classrooms are social spaces, and the language we use—inclusive of how we use pronouns as a power and identity politics—becomes a barrier we put up that positions ourselves as the ideal, the center, the focal point, and our students as subordinate objects relative to "us." When a white male basketball coach casually exclaims of his predominantly Black basketball team, "These boys could be playing much better than they are," what subconscious trauma is being imposed by "these" and "boys," given the historical racial tenor of Black men being called boys? When a white female educator cordially says of her primarily Black classroom, "You know I just love them, and their hugs," what amount of trauma is being reinforced by the othering politic of "them" and "their"? When educators unthoughtfully use possessive pronouns like "my" in signaling love for a classroom of beautiful kids, "my kids don't act like that," how might that possessiveness reify a power politic, particularly if a white educator is speaking about a group of Black and brown students?

One challenge that complicates the abolition of our oppressive use of pronouns, particularly "them" and "they," is the widened use of the two pronouns in the singular form as gender identities for non-binary—identifying as neither male nor female, and/or non–gender-conforming folx. I find myself against this wall, wrestling with how to hold in relationship the use of pronouns for all of my queer, non-white, non-binary, agender, and/or transgender students whose intersectionality is at the heart of lived experience, and abolish the oppressive implications that come along with "they" and "them." For all of our intersectional students, "they" functions as a means of power, protest, and resistance in navigating everyday life, and is therefore crucial to honor the function of gender-specific language. Crucial to *any* abolitionist project of emancipating ourselves from oppressive uses of language is recognizing that the abolition of "they" and "them" will inevitably impact how educators communicate with Black queer folx. Therefore, this radically humanizing response of emancipating our language invites Black folx with intersectional queer identities to create new, innovative identity markers that reject all pronouns, but never rejecting human dignity—a task of resistance and reconstruction.

Not only can aspiring abolitionists emancipate ourselves of the oppressive use of pronouns, but we can also commit to talking about systemic racism, not personal agency. The system or the person, who is to blame? Abolitionists committed to communal consciousness must not wrestle with that question relative to the consequential traumas of sociocultural, sociopolitical, and socioeconomic crises in the nation. Students suffering anxiety as a result of mass shootings in teaching and learning spaces is not the result of an individual, but the result of a system of poor gun control laws, allowing individuals of all socioemotional states access to unnecessary militarized weapons. Children detained in chains and cages, being maltreated at the southern border is not the blame of a singular individual, but the result of systemic xenophobia, antediluvian immigration laws, and white-supremacist nationalism. Black bodies—male bodies, female bodies, and trans bodies—being disproportionately over-policed, brutalized, and murdered routinely while being recorded by phones and body-cameras alike is not an individual problem, but a systemic consequence of America's chattel slave legacy. Black folx having to justify our experiences bird-watching in Central Park, exercising in a corporate gym, barbecuing in public gathering spaces, spray-painting our properties, selling water on the sidewalk, napping in the common area of our university dorm, and waiting patiently to pick up our children is not the result of any individual "Karen," but is the result of a systemic undervaluing of Black identity, rooted in a constitutional amendment recognizing us as 3/5ths a person.

Against that backdrop, crises of all proportions that have sociocultural, socioemotional, sociopolitical, socioeconomic, and socioenvironmental impact on our teaching and learning communities provide us as abolitionist leaders with an opportunity to talk to students and educators about the sin of systemic racism against Black folx, not the white wonder with individual Black agency. When white school leaders neglect the responsibility to talk about the function of racism as embedded within the fabric of sociopolitical and sociocultural structures—education, criminal justice, employment, income, housing, food, and healthcare—or remain silent about the history of structural racism, it gives white educators the permission to use language presuming that "really good, really successful" Black folx are exempt from the impact of racism. The teaching, learning, and classroom culture in cities and towns where structural racism goes unpacked, undiscussed, and even unacknowledged is the byproduct of the systemic privilege of whiteness, not the individual racism of KKK'ers, blue-lives-matter'ers, white-lives-matter'ers, all-lives-matter'ers, and make-America-great-again'ers—though each of those individual groups is an embodiment of the hegemony within the system itself. As such, an abolitionist approach to radically humanizing trauma is to resist the imposition of white-supremacist influence by acknowledging that even those we exclaim as notable—King,

X, Morrison, Hughes, Ali, Angelou, Baldwin, Franklin, Winfrey, Obama, and Knowles-Carter—despite their personal agency of diligence, effort, aptitude, and charisma, existed and exist within a structure of systemic racism. When school leaders focus rhetoric on the individual agency of our students, namely Black students, without naming that Black folx as a community exist within a structure designed to dismantle our effort and aptitude, school leaders perpetuate the oft-told alternative fact of an individual American Dream while ignoring the oft-experienced Black communal reality of an American Nightmare. To emancipate Black students of the trauma of assuming that individual agency, individual ethic, individual decency, individual code-switching, and individual compliance are the panacea to an emancipated life, abolitionists—aspiring and arrived—have to emancipate our rhetoric by centering systemic racism as a harm that individualism does not alleviate.

Immediately after graduate school, I joined an Independent boarding school in New England as the only—yes, only—Black male on staff, with a campus of more than 600 students and more than 70 staff members. I was dean of student life, a faculty member in the Upper School, and a dorm parent for a group of beautifully rambunctious, compassionately comical, and radically curious boys from all over the world. Before this, I had taught in two Independent day schools, where I had the disillusioning honor of being the only Black male on staff, so the induction period was succinct. As the recently on-boarded, energetically relational, linguistically "articulate" (you already know what that means), and unapologetically Black administrator with the freshly printed, ornately framed Harvard degree, faculty members swooned in the most trivial dialogues. In the dining hall one evening, a colleague and I were discussing whether or not Horace Mann's proposition was true that "education, then, beyond all other devices of human origin, is a great equalizer of the conditions of [wo]men—the balance wheel of social machinery."

Without any thought, she contended,

> I tell our kids, especially our kids from New York City [the school participated in a program that recruited Black boarding students from New York City] that this is one of the most equalizing experiences of their life; because even though we have kids here paying $50,000 a year, and *they* aren't paying that, *they* are having an equal experience.

I paused her and asked two questions.

> How do you know that "*they*"—the plurality of all Black students from New York City—aren't paying $50,000 a year? And, when you say that our Black students utilizing financial aid are having an equal experience as students of disproportionately-higher socioeconomic status, from Los Angeles to Oaxaca to Martha's Vineyard to London to Mumbai, what equalizes the experience?

Her face reddened as she replied, "Well, in the classroom, none of that matters. When students come into my classroom [she taught Upper School history], they are equal; they aren't their socioeconomic status, they aren't their race, and they aren't where they come from."

After a few seconds of reflection, I replied in an inadvertent diatribe,

> Tell me this. How exactly is that possible? How are students able, at 11, 12, 13, 14, and 15 years old [the school was a 6–9th boarding community], to disassociate identities, familial structures, lived experiences, academic backgrounds, socioeconomic realities, and social contexts for 50-minutes, three times per week, while in *your* classroom? Do our Indian seventh-graders walk in and intentionally detach the national influence of the

> British Raj—the period of imperialism when India was under control by the British on the Indian subcontinent from 1858 until 1947—on the language, government, and economics of the continent from their reading of the Indian Rebellion of 1857? Does a Black, apartment-living, working-class, Bronx-reared 13-year old have an equal educational experience—funds of knowledge, criticality, cultural capital, and social exposure—at a predominantly non-white, conservatively-principled, suburban boarding school, as a white, colonial-dwelling, upper-class, Vineyard-reared 13-year old? Both have equal dignity, but both do not have equal educational access.

After all of that, she still replied, "I just mean that, with a good education, we can all make it in America. Look at you, look at me. We both made it."

Knowing the vulnerability of positional politics as the newest hire, and being the only Black male, I begrudgingly took a safer route in response.

> I want to be inordinately clear. First, *our* navigation of the American education system is systemically distinct. Secondly, 'look at you, look at me' assumes that you are the Vineyard-formed and I am the Bronx-formed? Thirdly, as history faculty, it is incumbent upon you to situate your proposition of 'we all can make it' within the context of the inherent inequalities and systemic inequities embedded in the very fabric of American education, from finances to facilities. And once you've situated in that context, then you must reflect on the vast and ever-widening income disparities between Black folx and white folx when you control for educational attainment. So, the next time you propose that education is the great equalizer, be clear to also name education as the great oppressor. And let's be dismally honest, we will never be

equals in the sight of this nation, which was the intent of the founding fathers and the constitution.

To radically humanize the trauma of our students as a mean of power, the seemingly innocent rhetoric of aspiring abolitionists needs to stop its bend toward thoughtlessness and negligence and individualism and sensationalism, and bend the arc of rhetoric toward intention and systemic justice and inclusion and communal consciousness. And as a first step toward that bend where it results in the emancipation of language, school leaders must cultivate a culture of communal-resistance where perceptive attention is given to how educators, particularly our white educators, use linguistic power—in casual and calculated forms—to impose trauma on Black students; and therefore, invite all members of the community to participate in the resistance movement of calling linguistic power out, and calling folx who perpetuate it in. Of all the human consequences of our words in times of crisis, the greatest is that we will either retraumatize our students' confusion, dejection, grief, and hopelessness, or we will co-create the healing of our students *with* our students by offering words of clarity, healing, joy, and hope.

Embody the Centering of Relationships

As our nation continues to make sense of the trauma imposed on our individual and communal consciousness, compounded by us navigating the perpetual murders of Black bodies, at midnight on July 31, 2020, we were gifted with the creative genius and performative brilliance of Beyoncé Knowles-Carter through her visual album, "Black is King." As a treatise on Blackness—the color, the people, the idea, the life—Beyoncé co-opts the sociocultural narrative of the color's association with gloom, mourning, darkness, and evil, and reconstructs it as the fullness of beauty, richness, vitality, royalty, and enchantment. While our nation comes to terms with its treatment of Blackness, Black bodies,

Black communities, and Black students, Beyoncé exposes the world, a white world, to the pride, power, and possibilities of a people birthed from African Diaspora having survived the crises of the Middle Passage, American slavery, the Jim Crow South, and the presidential reign of Donald Trump. In effect, "Black is King" is a radically human, meaning-making treatment of the trauma imposed on Black folx, and the trauma often associated with the American oppression of Blackness.

But the splendor of "Black is King" has less to do with the individual creative-consciousness of Beyoncé, who is indisputably the luminary, and more to do with the radical centering of human relationships in the creation of the project, the framing of human trauma, and the holding of the story/ies being told. From Jay-Z to Tina Knowles-Lawson (her mother), to all three of her children (Blue Ivy, Rumi, and Sir), to Kelly Rowland, to Naomi Campbell, to Lupita Nyong'o, to Pharrell Williams, to lesser-American-known personalities like Salatiel, to Adut Akech, to Mr Eazi, to Busiswa, to Shatta Wale, to Moonchild Sanelly, to Wizkid, Beyoncé's gargantuan group of collaborators and special appearances underscores that a work of epic proportion is only actualized through relationships. More than the album itself, watching the credits was not only formidable, but it was mesmerizing. Name after name, after name, after name, after name, after name reinforced the centering of relationships. In fact, it accentuated the African proverb—"If you want to go fast, go alone. If you want to go far, go together." This Africanist perspective of "going together" underscores the role of collaboration and communal consciousness, which demonstrates that our capacity to reconstruct the inhumane and transform trauma is less about what we can do individually, challenging Western individualism, and more about what we can do when we center relationships.

At the start of any school year, teachers are often encouraged to build relationships with students in their classes, through questions about family structures, family walls, get-to-know-you worksheets and morning circles, artifact-sharing exercises, and the like. In structurally racist school readiness and professional development sessions, teachers, particularly white teachers, are admonished to get to know their "struggling students"—benevolent code typically reserved for the Black, brown, and/or economically-vulnerable ones. But when it comes to radically humanizing the integrated traumas that many, if not all, students are experiencing, the suggestion to "build relationships" is not only too ambiguous to be helpful, but it fails to go far enough. Instead of building relationships through questions like student interests, favorite colors, and television shows—in which the teacher remains the focal point as the one getting to know "the other"—centering relationships challenges one-way superficiality and equalizes the relationship for the teacher to have to expose themselves as much as they seek the exposure of the students. Beyoncé's treatment of Blackness was a relationship-centering treatment versus a relationship-building treatment in that she did not dehumanize the participation of the album's collaborators by subjecting African cultural practices and histories as "the other"; instead, she centered relationship by humanizing African cultural practices and histories as part of her own narrative. It was a mutual treatment of Blackness, not a subjecting treatment. Radically humanizing trauma invites the teacher to be as much of the subject in the relationship as the student, underscoring the idea that trauma and our inherent dignity *beyond* our traumas are a part of the human experience, regardless of our age and positional power. To be clear, this does not diminish the need for healthy, developmentally appropriate boundaries as to inhibit placing teacher-traumas on the student, but it does nuance those boundaries by humanizing the classroom through educators exposing parts of our inner truths as having been formed and informed by traumas without attempting to make our traumas equivalent to our students. Is there a fine line? Yes. But is that fine line worth walking? Yes. Why is it worth it? Because students know, intrinsically, when educators are committed to human-centered relationship.

As a school leader, prioritizing staff retention of highly effective, highly equitable, highly empathetic, highly relationship-centering teachers and staff is an embodiment of radically humanizing trauma. While it typically goes unnamed by students, I am without a doubt convinced that students, acutely in communities with disproportionate exposure to integrated traumas, track and analyze the revolving door of teachers and staff. At the end of the year, when staffing decisions are being made, how often does the leadership team ask itself, "What does this teacher represent relationally in the lives of our students for this community?" As students transition out of our classrooms and grades, and into their next stages, an abolitionist approach to transitions involves "rites of passage" where current teachers intentionally share meaning and knowledge crucial to the humanization of each student through meaningful, asset-based, relationship-centering stories of identity and dignity without the filter of judgment, data, or pretense.

For white folx, imagery like *The Blind Side*, *Freedom Writers*, *Green Book*, *Hidden Figures*, and, most nauseatingly, *The Help* will create a false correlation between relationship and saviorism. In cinema, this is the white saviorism trope, in which a well-meaning white person *builds* an unfolding relationship in order to rescue non-white, usually Black characters from oppressive plights. Without an abolitionist consciousness, white educators can often totter into the same trope, assuming that their role in the lives of Black students is to *build* a relationship in order to rescue students from perceived plights and poverties, versus centering relationships where they as educators are as much learners as their students are teachers. This teacher-student relationship-building trope dehumanizes the traumas that students bring into the classroom, particularly in periods of sociocultural and sociopolitical crises, because it obscures the role of relationship as a colonializing and civilizing tool, rather than a dignifying tool. Want to know how to identify white savior teaching as relationship-building? Listen for the language of power politics and social hierarchies through oppressive pronouns, "them" and "they" and "these," as white educators describe their relationships with Black students.

Even more than film, the most explicitly racist form of white savior relationship-building is the idea of mission trips—a staple of colonialism—where a group of white folx travel to foreign, non-white nations and territories, frequently places full of Black and brown folx, and give of their time, services, and monies with little regard to the inherent assets within the community. And the Instagram photos and stories demonstrate a faux-relationship where the white *helper* is passive in maintaining the oppressive structures, but often humbled and enlightened by an encounter with an indigenous, non-white community member. Does that model sound familiar? It should. Many popularized and noted teacher-pipeline programs like *Teach for America (TFA)* are often treated as two-to-three-year mission trips where predominantly white educators with access to time, educational privilege, and monies travel into urban, non-white cities and towns, frequently schools full of Black and brown students; and at the end of their mission, these educators leave the community rarely having centered relationship-building with students because of institutional commitments to "no excuses," sparse training, and a lack of abolitionist vision. As Dr. Chris Emdin, professor of science education at Columbia University notes, "… it [TFA] and programs like it tend to exoticize the schools they serve and downplay the assets and strengths of the communities they are seeking to improve."[13] One could argue, why critique programs attempting to close the teacher-shortage in our nation? That is inherently the wrong question to ask. In its place, the question is, what structural oppressions have produced a public education system in which people, namely people of color, are not entering into the teaching workforce? The integrated traumas that Black students are carrying would benefit most from experiencing abolitionist teachers, representative of the students who fill the seats in our classrooms, committed to radically humanizing the teaching and learning experience, while deconstructing the traumatizing practices *within* the classroom, instead of white folx exploiting Black and brown students to feel good about themselves and their contributions to the world. Without abolitionist school leaders calling out and calling in white educators who embody the centering of themselves, instead of the centering of relationships, when Black students are experiencing the traumas of crises, we risk an overdose of "I don't know what to say," "You have so much to be grateful for," "I don't see color," or "I understand what you're going through." Statements like these not only calcify student traumas, but they detrimentally oblige students to become the educators, having to guide white educators to realizations of trauma, race, and racism.

An abolitionist approach to centering relationship demands that school leaders and educators sit together with Black students (and families) in communities, not as saviors and suppliers, but as reflective listeners, recognizing that holding space for students (and families) to learn as much about us as humans as we learn about our students is a precondition and necessary abolitionist infrastructure for the healing and transformation of trauma. In effect, the abolitionist approach to radically humanizing trauma is about educators doing things with, and not for, our students on the journey of making sense and making meaning of the crises that plague all of our lives. Grounding our abolitionist approach in historical abolition, the "with" requires us as educators to metabolize and embody a new way of doing relationship, one where we participate fully, engage deeply, and reveal equally in the trauma transformation processes.

Practically, effective relationship-centering includes questions that both educator and student answer, story prompts that both educator and student tell, and artifact-sharing that both educator and student displays. Relationship-centering strategies include the cultivation of abolitionist ways of interacting with student, including listening to (and adjusting) one's tone of voice, being mindful of proximity (particularly in high-tension moments) as not to police Black bodies, avoiding the use of humor (as a de-escalation strategy when it is a façade for *our* lack of preparedness to engage, or potentially lessen the gravity of the moment), and knowing that, above all, holding space for students is about a relationship based on dignity, and not conditional on performance or ability or attendance or engagement. Radically humanizing trauma is about ensuring that each educational encounter is a mutual opportunity for students and educators to experience relationship-centering that invites all of us to make meaning, reinvent identity, and begin again.

Echoing the Resilience of Hope

How have Black folx, as a communal people, kept believing in this nation, generation after generation, as we've continued to experience the sociocultural and sociopolitical consequences of racism? How is it possible that Black folx have maintained trust in an American dream that will one day embody its constitutional ideals? How have Black families sustained belief in the promises and possibilities of a public education system that continually fails our children? How have Black mothers continued to birth Black children into a nation plagued by isms and phobias rooted in the moral fabric of its being? *Hope*.

Theorists, in all disciplines, have negligently appropriated the language of hope, only to abridge it to its emotional form as a way to conceptualize the world beyond our immediate plights and problems; or, it has been abridged to its religious sense of creating expectation for divine interference in the world. In effect, hope has been maltreated and misinterpreted as an end in itself. Although I am sympathetic to the notion of hope as an individual, socioemotional tool for navigating crises and traumas by seeing beyond them—foresight—as hope's end, the task of hope for Black folx transcends individualism, revolutionizing hope as a means to an actualizable end. Hope, like love and joy, for Black folx is more than an emotion. Hope, for Black folx, is more than a sensation. Hope, for Black folx, is more than an experience. Hope, for Black folx, is more than a mood. Hope, for Black folx, is more than a belief. Hope, I contend, is a methodological, communal, and generational tool of resilience that moves hope from being a passive noun to being a working verb. As abolitionists, we must consider hope as a strategic operative in any pursuit of freedom, which compels us to confront our most fundamental consideration as educators—for students, what hope is for.

In our teaching and learning communities, hope must become a resilience tool, by which we partner with students in reorienting our focus and conversation from the present-nature of crises and traumas as means to an end that we must make use of, to focus and conversation on the future-nature of a world without the crises and traumas that demanded hope in the first place. As Miyazaki offers, "… the power of hope as a method rests on a prospective momentum entailed in anticipation of what has not-yet become."[14] Underlying this proposition is the idea of momentum, which in physics is the impetus, driving force, and velocity gained by the development of a process or a course of movement. Hope, therefore, abandons itself as end, but stresses the essential nature of moving toward an end that has not yet been realized. In effect, hope is an ongoing tool of resilience that has only completed its task when the anticipation of what has not-yet become—freedom for all oppressed people, the transformation and meaning-making of trauma, and the healing of integrated traumas. At the intersection of Black oppression and our classrooms, hope emerges as a method of imagining, constructing, evaluating, and reconstructing the world as a continual cycle until all oppressed folx have been freed from the limits of prejudiced possibility in our democracy. In other words, an abolitionist introduction of hope into our pedagogy, our classroom norms, our school culture, and our adult learning communities reorients our effort from responding to what binds students to imagining who and what we will, can, and ought to be beyond captivity. Call to mind the ninth rhythm of an abolitionist approach, rooted in the words of James Baldwin that "hope is invented everyday."

The invention of hope, as an everyday enterprise, stresses the significance of human agency, without diminishing the impact of systemic oppression. Without intentionality on our parts as educators, and more explicitly white educators, the role of our students' human agency in the construction of hope will be overstated, diminishing the haunting effect of racism on and in the lives of our students. That is to say, hope as a working verb must be moving in the direction, with velocity, of constructing its ideal, while maintaining in sight the realities of what it is moving beyond.

If you can, imagine the *Sankofa*, which is based on a mythical bird with its feet planted in a forward-direction, but its head turned backward with an egg in its mouth, symbolizing the future. For the Akan tribe, a West African people in Ghana, the idea of Sankofa is expressed as "se wo were fi na wosan kofa a yenky," which literally translates to mean, "it is not taboo to go back and fetch what you forgot."[15] With many interpretations of its symbolism, what is clear is that critical to our capacity to imagine and construct and move toward an abolitionist democracy is in being grounded in and connected to the systemic racist history that informs our imagination. Such an image of the *Sankofa* captures, with immaculate clarity, the duality of hope as a tool of resilience—it moves in the direction of constructing what is not-yet, while maintaining its vision on what has been. It sees reality and constructs ideal. It knows oppression and constructs freedom. It recognizes racism and constructs equality. Be clear, hope is not satisfied with the present, but it also does not reject its existence. Thus, the resilience of hope is based on the fact that by working toward "what has not-yet become," we—as a collective—restrain ourselves from yielding to the despair of *what is.*

As educators, then, we have a responsibility to partner with our Black students in the invention of a hope that is not satisfied with the presence of trauma and crisis, that does not reject their existence, and not their existence in an individual sense, but in a communal sense. With that in mind, the invention of hope is not individual work, but communal work, and therefore, the vision "of what has not-yet become" is not an individual vision, but a communal vision. What does that mean for our students? It means partnering with our students, as a practice of abolitionist pedagogy, to co-vision and co-create the world as a community. As a people who have suffered the effects of American individualism, we must rebuff the use of hope to extend those effects, and instead use hope to move students in the direction of cultivating a communal consciousness where the language of "we hope" transcends "I hope." The more we expose and partner with our students to create a collective hope as a tool of resilience, the less likely our students, namely our Black students, will be to tolerate ideologies of subjugation and oppression from any source. By merely inviting students to do the active work of imagining and actualizing as a whole classroom with no singular individual at the foreground, students themselves will become abolitionists in pursuit of universal emancipation. This teaching and learning invitation is what bell hooks calls "pedagogies of hope."[16]

When I was teaching ninth grade at the boarding school, we often engaged in conversations around current affairs, in part because of the cognitive diversities in a classroom of nine to twelve boys from all over the world. In August 2012, the boys were pressed to talk about the shooting at a Sikh temple in Oak Creek, Wisconsin, where a white supremacist, Michael Page, murdered six innocent lives. One of my students, Yohan, identified as Sikh from Mumbai, and many of the boys were grieved and confused at the thought of someone murdering people on the basis of their religion, particularly given the boys' affection for a classmate who identified with the targeted, oppressed people. Michael, a thoughtful white student from Boston, remarked, "Mr. Harvey, I hope white supremacy comes to an end. Not only does it make all white people look like racists, but what they believe about people of color is baseless." Without any hesitation, Yohan replied, "*We* hope white supremacy comes to an end." Michael agreed, thanked him for the amendment, and restated his hope for a future world. I replied, "If that is our collective hope, what must we do to see it in the world? What is our responsibility in seeing the end of white supremacy?" From that point of departure, each one of the boys added to our communal consciousness of the world beyond, and ultimately without, white supremacy.

It is quite possible that for many of our students, our teaching and learning communities, our schools, and our classrooms are the closest proximity to the invention of hope. As abolitionists, using our classrooms to cultivate a future-oriented focus on freedom that is grounded in the systemic realities of American racism, we reverberate a resounding echo of hope that is centuries old, emanating from the abolitionism of Douglass and Tubman and Garrison and Grimké and Stowe and Truth and Brown. Our communal survival of America's past traumas, our communal radical-humanization of integrated traumas, and our communal imagination of a world without racial trauma and oppressive crises are the result of our abolitionist claim to hope.

For lo, the way is dark;
Through mist and cloud I grope,
Save for that fitful spark,
The little flame of hope.[17]

Notes

1. Dr. Eddie Glaude, the James S. McDonnell Distinguished University Professor of African American Studies at Princeton, in conversation with Dr. Cornel West, professor of the practice of public philosophy at the Harvard Divinity School. Simon, Clea. (2020). "Lessons from James Baldwin on betrayal and hope." *The Harvard Gazette*. Retrieved from https://news.harvard.edu/gazette/story/2020/07/james-baldwin-as-seen-against-the-backdrop-of-racial-upheaval/.

2. Bustamante, Jaleesa. (2019). K-12 School enrollment & student population statistics. Retrieved from educationdata.org/k12-enrollment-statistics/.
3. Eyerman, Ron. (2001). *Cultural Trauma: Slavery and the Formation of African American Identity*. Cambridge: Cambridge University Press, 2.
4. Eyerman, 2.
5. Lorde, Audre. (2007). "The Master's Tools Will Never Dismantle the Master's House" (1984). In *Sister Outsider: Essays and Speeches*. Berkeley, CA: Crossing Press, 2.
6. Miller-Karas, Elaine. (2015). *Building Resilience to Trauma: The Trauma and Community Resiliency Models*. New York: Routledge, 13.
7. Allen, Jon G. (1995). *Coping with Trauma: A Guide to Self-Understanding*. Washington, DC: American Psychiatric Association Publishing, 14.
8. Struzziero, Maria Antonietta. (2019). "Art Made Tongue—Tied by Authority: Art, Power, and Ideology in Julian Barnes's *The Noise of Time*." In *Language, Power, and Ideology in Political Writing: Emerging Research and Opportunities*, Onder Cakirtas, Ed. Hershey, PA: IGI Global, 47.
9. Salecl, Renata. (1998). *(Per)versions of Love and Hate*. London: Verso, 122.
10. Salecl, 120.
11. Salecl, 121.
12. Haas Institute for a Fair and Inclusive Society. (2018). "Object to Subject: Three Scholars on Race, Othering, and Bearing Witness." In *Othering and Belonging Journal: Expanding the Circle of Human Concern*, Issue 3, Andrew Grant-Thomas Ed. Berkeley: University of California.
13. Emdin, Christopher. (2016). *For White Folks Who Teach in the Hood … and the Rest of Y'all Too: Reality Pedagogy and Urban Education*. Boston, MA: Beacon Press, 7.
14. Miyazaki, Hirokazu. (2004). *The Method of Hope: Anthropology, Philosophy, and Fijian Knowledge*. Stanford, CA: Stanford University Press, 14.
15. Divine, David, Ed. (2007). *Multiple Lenses: Voices from the Diaspora Located in Canada*. Newcastle, NE: Cambridge Scholars Publishing, 172.

16. hooks, bell. (2003). *Teaching Community: A Pedagogy of Hope*. New York: Routledge, 9.
17. Dunbar, Paul Laurence. (1915). *The Complete Poems of Paul Laurence Dunbar*. New York: Dodd, Mead and Company, 98.

4

Knowing People and Place: Strategic Planning for Communal Consciousness

Of all the American adages we have likely espoused at some point in our personal or professional lives, there are seven words that reverberate more than any other: "failing to plan is planning to fail." As school leaders, we understand the function of planning, though we often focus our efforts and energies on lesson-planning; and with the same depth of consequence that lesson-planning is indelibly a critical component of effective teaching and learning, crisis-planning, trauma-planning, and equity-planning are critical components of an abolitionist approach to developing and maintaining a communal consciousness. Planning inevitably exhausts more time and energy than we tend to have as school leaders, likely because we are reacting to intersecting difficulties that beleaguer our days, weeks, and months. It requires you to deliberately suspend the normalcy of your schedule in order to imagine what has not yet arrived. Planning requires imagination. Planning, like *hope*, as a practice of the imagination—the faculty of seeing (in our minds) what we yet to see (with our-eyes)—is not a passive act, but a dynamic act, particularly as a tool of anticipatory leaders. "Leadership is both new and old, a timeless concept that must simultaneously reflect the times *yet stay ahead of them*. To do so is no small feat, but it is most worth of pursuit in contemporary organizational life."[1] Staying ahead of the times is a result of exercising the imagination as a future-planning tool; and abolitionist leaders who are committed to cultivating a communal consciousness are unafraid of, but discontented with, the lack of imagination because our duty is to see what is possible, including the possibility of crisis.

We are not the first generation to undergo an intersection of crises in a single cultural moment, with race and racism at the forefront and foreground. Thus, our ability to employ an abolitionist approach to anticipatory school leadership must be situated within, and understood as part of, the larger context of abolition, most notably the Underground Railroad. Though familiar through social, cultural, and political references, the Underground Railroad is latent with misconstructions, as noted by Dr. Francois in chapter 2, which have contributed to a reduced analysis of its function as a strategic, preemptive tactic. Without looking to the past, we could find ourselves shouldering unwarranted anxiety by assuming that we lack guidance in our planning. Enslaved Africans escaping the subjugation of slavery dates back to the 1500s when Black folx escaping south to what was known then as Spanish Florida was a common route and continued until the 1850s when enslaved Black folx—on southern plantations, distrustful of the involvement of self-proclaimed, altruistic white folx—would begin escaping north in pursuit of freedom. Yet the common thread from the 1500s to the 1850s was the systematically organized approach of most escapes—a communally conscious system of freedom organized and managed by Black folx—guided by an experienced knowledge of people and place. With the risks of being caught, beaten, tortured, and returned lingering as a shadow along the journey, escape demanded a high faculty of skill, knowledge, and strategy, which often took months, or even years of *planning* and reconnoitering.[2] Moreover, abolitionists understood that the communal freedom of enslaved Black folx could only be attained through communal planning, strategizing, and plotting. When Frederick Douglass planned his escape from slavery to the north, it was a community of folx from his Sabbath school who co-created the plan with him.[3] But here's what you must accept as an absolute: all planning has embedded risks, and will habitually fail us, just as planning failed abolitionists in our history. The issue of strategic planning in preparation for crises that will impose traumas on our communal consciousness is far too complex, puzzling, and mysterious for any of us to "get it right" every time. Hence, the abolitionist morality of planning is in the attempt, not the success.

Take April 15, 1848, when more than seventy enslaved Black folx in the Georgetown area of Washington, DC, attempted to board a ship named *Pearl*, owned by a white abolitionist named Daniel Drayton.[4] It took months of planning in partnership between Drayton and a group of newly escaped Black folx, not only as an effort to benefit others who were enslaved but to ignite a tremor in the nation's capital, shining a brighter light on the humane injustices of enslavement. More than skill, knowledge, and strategy, the *Pearl* Incident's planning required centering and upholding the human enterprise of escape, of freedom, of abolition. Abolitionists understood that more than escape routes, linguistic codes, mysterious subversions, and clandestine symbols, the strategic planning of abolition was a human task—fueled by humans, in partnership with humans.

Planning to Deepen Our Care—A Human Task

In the same way, schools are powered by humans in service of, and in partnership with, humans. An abolitionist approach to planning demands that schools, and school leaders, should be exercising our strategic imagination on how to plan with humans in mind and how to ensure that the humans within the community have the resources and tools requisite to continue advancing the community. At the intersection of a global pandemic, an economic downturn, and racial reckoning, during which corporations felt pressure to accelerate technological engagement and process automation, teaching and learning communities were pressured to accelerate our radical humanization through technology. The critical distinction within those strategic planning processes is that one focused on the technology itself, and the other focused on how that technology added to, enhanced, or revolutionized the human experience. From March 2020 teaching and learning communities of all kinds, namely PreK-12 schools, colleges, and universities, witnessed and experienced on-the-job-training in exponential change management. In a matter of hours, days, and, for some, weeks, unplanned crises impacting all aspects of American society forced changes that led to more changes, then more changes, often without time to pause, reflect, and assess on how to proceed without it being time for yet another change. The rapid nature of change amidst a crisis is inevitable, and therefore, we must expand our process planning, resource planning, and operational planning. But more than expanding our planning to account for rapid change, we must account for rapid trauma—in students, families, teachers, staff, and communities. Teachers and students are the two primary stakeholders that have the capacity to turn our teaching and learning communities upside down. Without deepening how we plan to care for and hold them in crises, we are, in effect, asking for disruption that extends beyond the initial shockwave of crisis. As school leaders, we must consistently be asking ourselves and our teams how we are radically humanizing our teaching and learning communities for those who center our mission, i.e. students, and those who fulfill our mission, i.e. teachers.

At its zenith, all of our planning is less about answers, and more about questions. Asking the right questions with the right group at the right time is core to the strategic planning process.

Therefore, school leaders who fail to ask questions are leaders who are planning to fail to students, families, teachers, staff, and communities. Zora Neale Hurston in her notable 1937 work, *Their Eyes Were Watching God*, offers in literary magic the worth of preemptive planning through the voice of her narrator. She writes, "There are years that ask questions and years that answer."[5] As leaders committed to an abolitionist approach, Hurston's words, if we allow them to, extend an invitation to ask difficult questions and pursue clarity in the midst of the crises around us. As disconcerting of a proposition as it may be, there are years when we will lack answers to the pressing and perplexing questions of racism, social injustice, community unrest, epidemiological pandemics, and economic recessions. It is in those years wherein we lack answers that we must show the courage to question, because it is our questions that frame our planning.

Before we begin our due diligence of asking questions involving our sociopolitical, sociocultural, socioeconomic, and socioenvironmental contexts, we must commit to a series of questions that form and inform how we deepen our care for students and teachers—our socioemotional context—with an abolitionist approach.

Socioemotional

1. What is one practice in our teaching and learning community that focuses on "fixing" humans—students, teachers, and staff—rather than fixing the conditions that marginalize humans? And upon identifying *one* practice, how can we reshape that practice to accomplish one or more of the abolitionist rhythms?
2. What do we ask, expect, or demand of our students, teachers, staff, and families—formally and informally—that might be implicitly and explicitly oppressive, particularly for subjugated identities, even if we do not intend to be oppressive/racist?

3. For which areas, and how often, do we invite and expect student voices, family voices, and teacher voices before making practice, policy, protocol, process, and programming decisions within our teaching and learning community? Correspondingly, do we *impose* more than we *query*?
4. How do we consistently, *humanely*, and *ethically* center the psychological and emotional wellness of our students, teachers, staff, and families beyond retroactive social-emotional lessons in response to a classroom conflict, morning meeting words of the week where we introduce value-vocabulary, emotion-identifying charts and classroom corners with plush pillows, and IEP-mandated social work 1:1 and small group sessions?
5. When we recruit for and hire *who* is responsible for caring for and holding our students in times of crises, what identities, histories, traumas, biases, and assumptions do we know exist within those who are called (or staffed) to do the caring? And how will we control for any known biases and assumptions, implicit or explicit, within those staff members *before* they care for our students?
6. What are the mental health trends and mental illnesses rates within our community? How do these rates align to the rates we experience within our teaching and learning community? What are the leading causes, sources, and triggers of mental illnesses within our community? And how do those causes, sources, and triggers of trauma manifest in various identity groups?
7. How do students, families, and teachers discuss mental health, trauma, and access to mental healthcare? In what ways do *we* center conversations about mental health as a teaching and learning community? How do we normalize dialogue about mental illnesses without normalizing the consequences of mental illnesses?
8. In what ways does our teaching and learning community, through our practices, policies, protocols, and/or processes, either participate in the perpetuation of or

the healing of traumas and mental illnesses within our community?

9. As a teaching and learning community aspiring to pursue an abolitionist approach to all that we do, can we live with, and are we prepared to live with, the consequences of failing to care for and hold our students, teachers, staff, and families?
10. What do we hope to achieve as a teaching and learning community when we make space to care for and hold our students, teachers, staff, and families? In effect, what outcomes matter most to us?

While the ninth question is loaded with moral implications for planning, the tenth question is the medium and stimulus for shaping your planning. With passive consideration, the tenth question probably reads straightforward, and as a school leader, you may think you already know what you hope the outcomes are for students and teachers while being cared and held by the community, particularly in crisis. In the spirit of abolition, what *you* hope the outcomes are is immaterial, because abolitionist care and abolitionist holding are about the entire community being clear on what the outcomes are while folx are being cared for and held. As such, this question, more than the other nine, demands that school leaders ask every stakeholder group within the community in order to align the practices and programming of care with the imagined and communicated outcomes for care. By understanding the full, and at time competing, spectrum of priorities for deepening the human and humane work of caring for the community, abolitionist leaders position the community to deepen and expand its impact.

Planning to Learn Our Place—An Operational Task

In 2013, one of my mentors and the president of Simmons College of Kentucky, Dr. Kevin W. Cosby, told me, "Know your place. If you don't know your place, you won't know your

.f you don't know your people, you aren't *leading well.*" ı that place and knowledge intersect as the grounds for leading well stresses the abolitionist idea that doing the work of learning *place*—environment, politics, culture, social norms, and economics—is directly connected to doing the work of learning *humanity*—emotion, imagination, and freedom. For that reason, we must lead our school communities anticipatorily, proactively, and preemptively by probing our understanding of place—the sociopolitical, sociocultural, socioeconomic, and socioenvironmental conditions that contextualize our teaching and learning communities. In effect, the ability to cultivate, maintain, and/or deepen communal consciousness in a crisis is the difference between reactionary and anticipatory understanding of the place in which our school communities are situated; and what distinguishes reactionary and anticipatory understanding of the place is planning, or vice versa, failing to plan. By understanding and anticipating the socio-conditions that impact, influence, and inform our school community, the arrival of a crisis does not initiate a period of reactionary learning, but a period of contemplative responsiveness.

As teaching and learning leadership pushes us deeper into isolation from other teaching and learning leaders, communities, and organizations—that is, working in a bubble intentionally and unintentionally from others who do this work—one of the consequences is the growing superficiality of our understandings of the place in which we lead. In effect, the more we isolate ourselves in this work of leading schools, the more we isolate ourselves from the knowledge necessary to lead well. This is part of the danger of what I call "commuter abolition," which is the practice of teaching and learning leaders commuting *into* places with a sense of compassion, which compels a drive for abolitionist work, while also barring themselves from the lived experiences of that work by commuting home, often in neighborhoods and communities that have distinct privileges and resource from the ones they are leading. In effect, there are two levels of learning place: *place-based abolition* and *commuter abolition*. Neither is morally superior, yet each has varied degrees of abolitionist efficacy and communal credibility. When making critical decisions about relocating for my present role, leading a network of charter schools in East Harlem, I had to decide where I would live. Was I going to engage in commuter abolition, or would I situate myself in the nucleus of the place where I would be leading a network of schools toward abolitionist ideals? I recalled those words, "Know your place. If you don't know your place, you won't know your people. If you don't know your people, you aren't *leading well*." Place-based abolition was my choice, and has been integral to cultivating and leading with a communal consciousness.

In learning an organization's *place*, established nonprofit and business-focused leadership suggests a series of pragmatic, operational, financial, and human capital questions a leader must ask in order to preemptively position an organization to lessen its risk and vulnerability in crisis.[6] Those questions matter. But an abolitionist approach to communal consciousness demands an equally consequential series of sociopolitical, sociocultural, socioeconomic, and socioenvironmental queries, which at the heart situates the teaching and learning community within its place-based context as the underpinning of planning. In this age of heightened compartmentalization and isolationism, school leaders are tasked with planning for and with the school as both the center of focus and a site situated in the broader context of its location. Therefore, it is crucially important to remember that developing and sustaining a teaching and learning community with a communal consciousness demand an ethos where the center of focus is the school, but this cannot come at the expense of understanding the place in which the school is situated. Hold in mind the abolitionist rhythm: an abolition approach intentionally integrates people and place, recognizing that the pursuit of freedom for all oppressed identities demands an understanding of the ways that identities are formed by, and inform, the place in which those identities are situated. Therefore, the web of destiny that points toward freedom is not people over place, or place over people, but people and place mutually.

The long-term sustainability of a shared sense of solidarity in the pursuit of universal freedom depends prominently on the school leader's level of people *and* place. By learning place, leaders committed to abolition can demonstrate a deferential, asset-based approach to our roles, accepting an oft-neglected truth, which is that the places in which we lead have far more knowledge to offer us than we have to offer the places. The following five sections of questions are not intended to be definitive for learning place, but are meant to provide an inquiry framework for leaders, namely commuter abolitionists, who are situated outside of the boundaries of *the place* in which they lead.

Sociocultural

Each aspect of how we as people interact with the place in which we are situated is shaped, informed, and conceived through a series of real and perceived social systems and social structures, cultural symbols, and cultural knowledge. Creating our sense of place, then, is how we make meaning of the intersection of society and culture in order to "mediate and regulate our relationships with others and with ourselves," thus sociocultural inquiry.[7] The way we make meaning of our community, locate ourselves within that community—individually and relationally—and navigate that community in meaningful and productive, or unproductive, ways is through the connections we create between social and cultural factors. In many ways, the sociocultural context for a teaching and learning community is the most pronounced context for its students.

1. Who are the primary racial and ethnic groups within our community? How long have the identified racial and ethnic groups had a presence in the community, and under what conditions? And what is the current state of relations between identified racial and ethnic groups?

2. What are the unspoken, unwritten norms of how people operate within the community? What do we see and hear that gives us a sense of the social and cultural forms of power within our community?
3. When people organize and come together at a large scale, what kinds of social and cultural realities catalyze those gatherings? Where do the gatherings take place, and why do they take place there?
4. Is our community known for, influenced by, or committed to religious participation? If so, what religious communities are present and active? And how does religion form and inform how our people—students and families—interact with our teaching and learning community?
5. What histories and stories do people tell about our community—its successes, failures, missed opportunities, investments, and leadership? How do those histories continue to reinvent themselves presently, or how have those histories been revolutionized for progress, or regress?
6. How are homes and families organized within our community, and how do we know? What is the role of gender and sexuality in homes within our community, and how has our teaching and community interacted with the varying structures and definitions of home and family in our community?
7. Within our community, what relationships matter most to people? Do family, friendship, religion, economics, or other social and cultural factors we have seen or heard define those relationships? And how do those relationships demonstrate themselves in our teaching and learning community?

Sociopolitical

Abolition, historically and contemporarily, must be kept in context of the intersections that occur between social structures and political transformations. Any learning of place that will occur must involve knowledge of the political scope within a community, including legislation (and legislative history), policies, elected and appointed offices, traditions, and political events that define a community. Again, all teaching and learning are political, particularly in moments of crisis and heightened communal sentiment; and the exchange between politics and teaching and learning contributes to the structural inequalities, barriers to progress, or subjugation of freedom in within a community.

1. Who are the formal institutional/political leaders, community powerbrokers, and informal influencers within the community? And, within those three categories, who are the people who share two of those identities synchronously?
2. What do the formal institutional/political leaders, community powerbrokers, and informal influencers know about our teaching and learning community? Are any of those people formally and/or informally connected to us as a parent/caregiver, board member, donor, or alumni/ae? And what is the state of our, and the school leader's, relationship with those people who might connect?
3. Have we ever made use of, or requested, the brokering of power from any the aforementioned categories? If they offered their formal or informal power, did we fulfill our assurances in the agreement?
4. What policies, bills, and/or legislative discourse are a part of the structural inequity, resource inequity, or building/land inequity of our teaching and learning community? And are any of those policies, bills, and/or legislative discourse priority for engaging our formal institutional/political leaders, community powerbrokers, and informal influencers?
5. What key political events have impacted our teaching and learning community since our establishment? How have we educated our stakeholders of those key political events? And are there remnants of those events in the political ether that continually serve as a shadow to our abolitionist advancement?

6. How does our community tend to politically identify—individually and communally—lean, and vote? Do those voting trends align to the knowledge we have about our sociocultural context? How are those political affiliations working for and/or against us as a teaching and learning community? And who is defining whether they are working for and/or against us?
7. Which nonprofits and social service agencies are within the community, and what are their program areas of focus? How do those nonprofits and social service agencies partner with our teaching and learning community? What demographics within our teaching and learning community utilize the services of the identified nonprofits and social service agencies?
8. How have the nonprofits and social service agencies within the community demonstrated a commitment to the abolitionist rhythms? How have those nonprofits and social service agencies done the work of dismantling the systemic roots of the areas they address?
9. What types of political and social movements (or organizations) have been organized to address the leading political and social inequities and injustices facing our community? Do those movements reflect national issues, or mostly local issues? Who participates in the movements? And are the movements effective, according to the various stakeholders in our sphere of proximity—students, teachers, staff, and families?

Socioenvironmental

Place is place in both a contextual sense and a literal sense, in that it refers to and defines the immediate physical, environmental, epidemiological, and ecological settings in which our teaching and learning community is located, and in which the folx within our community are living, working, and doing life together. As abolitionists, we must be conscious that most of the prevailing inequities and injustices latent within oppressed communities are directly interconnected to socioenvironmental concerns. Further, any attempts at pursuing freedom for all oppressed folx in a teaching and learning community must be situated within socioenvironmental freedom, or else the literal place in which freedom occurs will re-oppress, re-subjugate, and re-enslave. In the earliest days of my superintendency, a commuter-abolitionist white colleague in another organization asked, with a heavy heart, "Are we in the food industry? Are we in healthcare? It feels like people expect schools to do everything, and I just don't see the connections to our mission." I replied by question, with grace, "Do you believe in freedom?" Freedom to hope without freedom to access food, healthcare, parks, and clean air is a hungry, sick, restricted, and respiratory-compromised freedom.

1. Where and what kinds of green spaces are located within the community? Are there parks? If so, what are various features that the parks offer for recreation, teaching, and learning? How do stakeholders within our community currently use green spaces? Do our stakeholders identify those green spaces as safe? And do we make use of those green spaces in our pedagogy?
2. What and where are the primary outdoor landmarks—socially, culturally, politically, religiously, and recreationally—in proximity to our teaching and learning community? Are those landmarks protected by city, state, or federal ordinance? And do we make use of those landmarks in our pedagogy?
3. Who are the primary food providers in the community? Is there access to fresh fruits and vegetables in supermarkets, street-stands, and/or farmers markets? If not, what has been our role in providing fresh fruits and vegetables to the households within our teaching and learning community?
4. What are the current and future transportation trends within our community? Are our students, staff, teachers,

and families reliant on public transportation? If so, is public transportation a priority budget-investment for our formal institutional/political leaders? How do we engage the transportation industry, i.e. providing public transportation passes, parking discounts, and/or other ways?

5. What is the state of public health within the community? Are clinics, hospitals, and healthcare centers, for the insured and non-insured, accessible within the community? Are there mental health resources, for the insured and non-insured, accessible within the community? How do we educate our stakeholders on the state of public health, including available resources, within our community?
6. What are the leading health disparities and wellness inequities within the community? Do our stakeholders regularly engage with, by sight or interaction, residents with drug- or alcohol-related sicknesses? Do any of our students or families have drug- or alcohol-related sicknesses that we are formally or informally partnering to address? If so, what would be the consequences if we ceased our partnership in addressing drug- or alcohol-related sicknesses with students and families?
7. Are our buildings equipped with clean drinking-water systems? If so, do we intentionally promote water consumption through refillable bottles, or do we participate in bottled-water purchasing and distribution? If our buildings are not equipped with clean drinking-water systems, have we lobbied our formal institutional/political leaders, community powerbrokers, and informal influencers?

Socioeconomic

Money matters—who has it (and who doesn't), how it flows, what systems control it, and who controls the systems. As school leaders, we typically limit our engagement with economics to the economics of our budgets and our buildings; as abolitionist school leaders, we must concern ourselves with the economics of our communities, and how economic activity affects and is shaped by social systems and structures. Our capacity to pursue freedom is directly connected to the progression, stagnation, or regression of the economy within our communities. What good is it to be free to hope, free to imagine, and free to think, but income insecure, job insecure, or economically oppressed? Dr. Martin Luther King, Jr. noted this incongruence in freedoms. He concluded that immediately after the Civil War, the formerly enslaved experienced "abstract freedom, since they found themselves with no bread to eat, no land to cultivate, no shelter to cover their heads."[8] In an abolitionist sense, the guiding socio-economic factors that determine freedom include—*employment, education, housing, and income*—all of which are typically related but not universally.

1. What are the leading industries and types of jobs within our community? Who are the top five largest employers within our community? What are those employers' risks of economic failure? How are the families within our teaching and learning community represented within those industries, jobs, and employers?
2. What is the distance (by percentage/by dollar amount) between the median income in our community, the national median income, and the median income in our teaching and learning community? What is the current state of income security and livable wages within our community?
3. How do the employment and unemployment trends, rates, and risks within our community, and within our teaching and learning community, reflect that of adjacent or proximate communities? What percentage of our community has access to disposable income? How do we calculate access to disposable income? What do we ask of families within our teaching and learning

community (e.g. uniforms, field trip fees) that expenses their income?

4. In what ways, through policies, practices, and programming, does our teaching and learning community perpetuate or exacerbate economic inequities? How are the economic inequities manifested in our teaching and learning community by identity factors, e.g. race, gender, household structure, and educational attainment?
5. What are the housing trends in our community? How are safe and secure housing options in our community relative to adjacent or proximate communities with similar demographics? How are the residential and transiency trends within our communities relative to adjacent or proximate communities with similar demographics? What are the housing conditions within our teaching and learning community, and how do those conditions impact our pedagogical approach?
6. Are our community, and/or adjacent and proximate communities, experiencing gentrification and its consequences, i.e. increased housing costs, redevelopment of community buildings into apartments and condominiums, and decreased rent-controlled/rent-stabilized/lower-income/public housing options? Within our community, and within our teaching and learning community, where do people move from, and where do they move?
7. What post-secondary academic pathways exist within proximity to our teaching and learning community? Of those post-secondary pathways, what percentages of our community stakeholders pursue each pathway, on average? Within our teaching and learning community, how many families have completed high school, traditional post-secondary credentials, i.e. degrees, certificates, and/or non-traditional post-secondary credentials, i.e. apprenticeships, micro-credentials?

Planning—What You Probably Had in Mind

Now, if you arrived at this chapter looking for a clearly defined strategic guide on planning for crisis, then you more than likely did not think about planning to deepen care and planning to learn place. Instead, and more conventionally, you were looking for a series of questions that, optimally combined, yielded the lowest level of risks for your teaching and learning community in the face of crises. The problem of starting with conventional strategic questioning, without laying the requisite abolitionist framework, is that crises, because they are unplanned and unexpected, have the tendency to cause school leaders to over-privilege strategic playbooks versus critical place-based analysis. In times of crises, particularly crises which threaten the stability and reputational well-being of our teaching and learning community, our impulse is often to begin solving short-term problems. When financial and operational survival is at risk, this approach is often deemed justified by external stakeholders, teachers, and staff, because individual consciousness arouses self-survival. It is, however, clear that an abolitionist approach is less concerned with short-term problem-solving, and more concerned with long-term thinking that pursues freedom for all oppressed folx within the community. In fact, short-term problem-solving is a symptom of hegemonic white supremacy, because it shifts our communal attention away from the work of sustainable abolition. That said, teaching and learning communities should engage in conventional strategic planning by asking critical operational and financial questions.

As an abolitionist community, every conventional strategic question put through the strategic planning inquiry-cycle, regardless of how pragmatic, should end with one of the following statements—of/for the oppressed identities in our community, of/for the subjugated and marginalized folx in our community, of/for the Black folx in our community, of/for income insecure folx in the community, and any other identity-centered closing. This is an exercise I call oppression testing. In oppression testing, every response to every strategic question is probed through the lens of oppression. The purpose of oppression testing is not to prove that the teaching and learning community is abolitionist, but, reversely, to demonstrate where the oppression within your systems, structures, and plans is pronounced. Maintaining a communal consciousness in times of crises requires us to oppression test all strategic questions not based on how it impacts an individual, but how it impacts a group of individuals and/or the entire community. It should be noted that oppression testing is not intended to be a practice of "othering," meaning it is not about treating oppressed folx as inferior, or as subgroups in the planning process; instead, oppression testing is about ensuring that every strategic plan is abolitionist in its approach by accounting for and responding to the sociopolitical, sociocultural, socioeconomic, socioemotional, and socioenvironmental needs within the teaching and learning community.

* good audit practice

Oppression Tests for Strategic Planning—An "Our" Imperative

1. How can our teaching and learning community ensure sustainable financing and stable cash reserves, while also meeting the socioemotional and socioenvironmental needs *of the oppressed identities in our community*?
2. How does our budget reflect the long-term sustainability of our teaching and learning community remaining as an effective, viable, and trusted organization *for marginalized and subjugated folx in our community?*
3. Have we considered the impact of a crisis in the budgeting and long-term revenue planning/forecasting processes, and implemented early warning mechanisms,

particularly for the potential impact on meeting the socio-emotional and socioenvironmental needs *of the oppressed identities in our community?*

4. Are there well-coordinated and standardized communication systems and protocols to ensure clear and transparent communication with all stakeholders, particularly *the technologically oppressed in our communities*?
5. When a crisis has significant financial impact, how can we adapt our teaching and learning delivery model to maintain (or reduce) costs, both in the short and medium term, while also meeting the socioemotional and socio-environmental needs *of the oppressed identities in our community?*
6. How will disruption impact our teaching and learning delivery in the short and medium term, and how will that disruption impact *income insecure folx in our community*?
7. What is our inventory of technological equipment and Internet bandwidth to meet the teaching and learning delivery needs of all of our students, particularly *the income and housing insecure students in our community*?
8. Is our teaching and learning delivery model resilient enough to recover from the impact of a crisis with a seamless 'new normal,' and manage potential crises in the future *that will disproportionately impact and compound the needs of socioeconomically insecure folx in our community*?

At the core of the oppression test is the use of "our," which is used to denote an inclusive communal approach to the strategic planning. For the sake of oppression testing, school leaders and leadership teams should be clear and bold in their planning to always use inclusive, plural pronouns that intentionally abolish the positional power politics between leaders and students and families, and intentionally place both groups in the same situational context. In strategic planning oppression testing—our, we, and us are abolitionist imperatives and linguistic non-negotiables.

What'll Be Is What'll Be—The Limits of Planning

One of my now deceased grandmother-figures, Gwendolyn Vaughn, once rebuked me by saying, "Do your part and trust your part, because what'll be is what'll be." Endemic to an abolitionist mindset is a desire to get it right every time, because the stake is high—*freedom and justice for all*. But it is important to note that even with the most judicious exercise of the imagination, the most critical question-based analysis, and the most oppression-tested strategic planning, there are limits to our capacity as school leaders in developing the foresight for crisis-planning. What'll be is what'll be. The nature of complex, integrated, and interdependent crises means that planning for uncertainty, ahead of uncertainty, quickly multiplies the moment any single factor within the planning process is altered. That point of changing factors often causes anxiety for school leaders, particularly fixed-mindset leaders, who find consolation and reassurance in a methodical approach to leadership. For this reason, an abolitionist approach to planning urgently demands that school leaders intentionally invest in developing an agile and growth-mindset—an ability to digest new information swiftly—and pivot our planning in response to that new information even faster than our digestion of it. By developing and exercising a growth-mindset as the mental model for our planning in times of crisis, we do *our* part as abolitionists; and after doing our part, we must trust our part, because when it comes to crisis, what'll be is what'll be.

Notes

1. Fairhurst, Gail & Connaughton, Stacey L. (2014). "Leadership: A communicative perspective." *Journal*, Vol. 10, No. 1, 24.
2. Franklin, John Hope & Schweninger, Loren. (1999). *Runaway Slaves: Rebels on the Plantation*. New York: Oxford University Press, 229.
3. Perry, Theresa, Steel, Claude & Hilliard III, Asa. (2003). *Young, Gifted, and Black: Promoting High-Achievement among African–American Students*. Boston, MA: Beacon Press, 17.

4. Ricks, Mary Kay. (2007). *Escape on the Pearl: The Heroic Bid for Freedom on the Underground Railroad*. New York: HarperCollins, 7.
5. Hurston, Zore Neale. (2006). *Their Eyes Were Watching God, 75th Anniversary Edition*. New York: HarperCollins. Originally published 1937.
6. Themudo, Nuno S. (2013). *Nonprofits in Crisis: Economic Development, Risk, and the Philanthropic Kuznets Curve*. Bloomington: Indiana University Press.
7. Lantolf, James P. (2000). "Introducing Sociocultural Theory." In *Sociocultural Theory and Second Language Learning*, James P. Lantolf Ed. Oxford and New York: Oxford University Press, 1.
8. Birt, Robert E. (2012). *The Liberatory thought of Martin Luther King, Jr.: Critical Essays on the Philosopher King*. Lanham, MD: Lexington Books, 166.

5

The Danger of Acting: Making Decisions as Acts of Resistance at the Risk of Resentment

One minute and forty seconds—*100 seconds*—after a 3:25:51pm takeoff from New York City at LaGuardia Airport, en route to Charlotte, for an eventual destination of Seattle, the flight was ordinary and unremarkable. And then, Captain Chesley "Sully" Sullenberger says aloud to his first officer, Jeffrey Skiles, "This can't be happening." On January 15, 2009, US Airways Flight 1549, an aircraft carrying 155 people—150 passengers and five crewmembers—lost both its engines 100 seconds after takeoff. What caused it? A double bird strike. At 3:27:11pm, a group of birds, Canadian geese, were sucked into both engine turbines, a rare incident. Flight 1549 was less than 3,000 feet in the air. Captain Sully, with more than thirty years of military and commercial fight experience, was experienced enough to know that there was very little possibility that at that height, the Airbus A320 was going to be able to land on a runway. Or even ground altogether. He had to make decisions, many of which resisted the logic and counsel of air traffic control, but which centered the humans on Flight 1549.

Patrick, the air traffic controller that day, "immediately began to try to get us back to a runway at LaGuardia," Captain Sully shared. Knowing that Patrick lacked the lived knowledge of being in that plane, in that moment, with minutes left and 155 lives hanging in the balance, Captain Sully and Officer Skiles *had to act*. At 3:29:20pm—two minutes and eighteen seconds after the birds strike, Captain Sully repeated himself to Patrick, but surer and resolute. "We're gonna be in the Hudson." Knowing that there would be resentment for that decision, lingering in the backdrop, Sully later reflected that his pursuit was clear, "making hard choices and sticking with them." His goal was singular and well-defined. "I was willing to sacrifice the airplane to save lives." Less than four minutes after its engines shut off, at 3:31pm, Flight 1549 landed on the Hudson River. All 155 people onboard that flight escaped alive, including Captain Sully. Ten years after that valiant moment, Captain Sully took to Twitter on January 17, 2019, and shared his account of acting, from a place of communal consciousness, to save the lives of those onboard.

The Foremost of All Acts

Abolition is about acting. It is about making decisions. But not just *any decisions*, decisions at philosophical, strategic, and operational levels. Abolitionist decisions at a philosophical level are grounded in what we, as leaders, believe about the world, our society, and the community in which we are situated. Abolitionist decisions at a strategic level are directly aligned with the priorities and objectives within the teaching and learning community. Abolitionist decisions at the operational level are those which allocate and implement resources, fiscal and human, that correspond to the strategic and philosophical decisions. In teaching and learning communities committed to cultivating a communal consciousness, our acting must transcend individualism, which is often at the forefront of making decisions in crisis. During crisis, when unpredictability is the canvas against which we are making sense of what is happening and how it will impact our communities, our acting is often a complex intersection of dangerous decisions, human dysfunctions, trauma coping, procedural ambiguities, communication stress, inadequate information, inconsistent details, role nuance, and unclear on where to begin.

As Flight 1549 was gliding downward, toward the Hudson River, Captain Sully offers the unconcealed secret of the first decision—naming that a crisis exist. "Mayday mayday mayday. Uh this is uh Cactus fifteen thirty nine hit birds, we've lost thrust in both engines we're turning back towards LaGuardia."[1] We'll talk about *how* you name it in the next chapter. For now, it is only important to note that often the hardest decision for leaders in crisis—and not in crisis—is to name when there is a problem. Whether or not we are protecting our individual ego, shielding our students and staff from panic, assuming we can fix it, or simply longing for it to dematerialize before anyone notices, school leaders often have to be convinced to name that a problem is brewing. It is a hard decision, our hardest decision, because it's a choice that demands that we look beyond ourselves as an individual, and look at the impact and implications of *not naming.* With thirty years of experience, Captain Sully could have delayed making the choice to signal, "Mayday," a distress call through radio communications made in life-threatening emergencies. He could have delayed to gain more clarity on the effects of the impact on the turbines. The question, then, is why didn't he wait? The explanation for this is quite simple. Humility.

In our conversations around the word, *humility*, we rarely invoke images of power and strength, intentionality and choice. We have developed a faulty understanding of humility as a reflexive, docile surrender to a thing that is bigger and more controlling than we are. I want to contend that humility, at its core, is not only a decision but also an abolitionist act of resistance. The same effect that we ascribe confidence and sureness has, as mechanisms for making choices, should be the same effect we credit to humility. What if we thought of crisis as an egotistical adversary? We could contend that crisis, because of inflated ego, would expect us to confront it with an overstated ego—giving it the same energy it gives us. But our strength is not always what it seems to be. Confronting crisis—unplanned and unexpected, oppressive and unjust—with humility is the way of abolition—a way that recognizes strength, not in self-centeredness and individual might, but strength in selflessness and communal responsibility. Captain Sully's ability to call "Mayday" was his strength, a strength based on his unyielding communal consciousness that he "was willing to sacrifice the airplane to save lives." On the one hand, naming that a crisis exists is the first decision; on the other hand, choosing humility, which is the source of our strength to name that a crisis exists, is the foremost of all choices.

Ronald Thiemann, a now deceased political theologian and one of my former professors at Harvard, would argue that humility, like courage and integrity, could not be taught in classrooms, but must be learned through experiences. For Thiemann, humility as a practice contained consequential truths for leading in society. I recall a conversation over coffee with a former instructional coach who was struggling to find their sense of place in his first year coaching lower school faculty, because he had primarily taught and coached upper school over the last ten years. When he'd see a Kindergarten or first-grade team moving toward a pedagogical crisis due to poor-planning or misplaced activities with the day's learning standards, he'd name it. But he was oft-met with resistance and even resentment. He couldn't make sense of why given his years of experience successfully coaching upper grades. Then, he said something that underscored why he consistently faced resistance.

"I mean, you'd think they'd appreciate me giving them a heads up. Most of them were still in school when I started teaching. Doesn't that count for something?" He said as he rolled his eyes and sipped his oat milk latte.

Wanting to uplift his confidence, while also inviting him to recognize his humility-gap, I replied. "Of course it counts for something, but is it the only thing that counts?" It was intended to be rhetorical. He replied.

"Well, I guess not! But we can't discount experience." He was growing frustrated.

> We can't, and we shouldn't—you're right. *And* [I stressed], we cannot assume that experience is enough to demand trust, respect, and understanding. You having years of experience as a teacher and a coach give you particular and pointed insight to see what novice teachers often neglect to see. *And*, you must acknowledge that your years of experiencing in teaching and coaching were limited to upper school, which means that the teachers you are now coaching know more than you know about their content areas, the brain development of younger students, and potentially *how* to teach them. In effect, there is as much to learn from them, as there is as much to coach. And when you don't approach the acts of your coaching—naming potential problems and recommending solutions—with humility, you are deserving of resentment.

When I find myself in a post-observation debrief with principals, assistant principals, instructional coaches, or directly with teachers (which is a rare occurrence these days) that conversation about humility resonates. As such, part of our observational debriefs protocol, particularly when against the backdrop of a crisis, is to intentionally ask and answer: *what did you learn anew, what did you know that was expanded, what did you think you knew that was deconstructed, or what did you learn about yourself?* By asking any or all of the previously mentioned questions, you allow yourself to continually learn and practice humility as the foremost of all abolitionist actions.

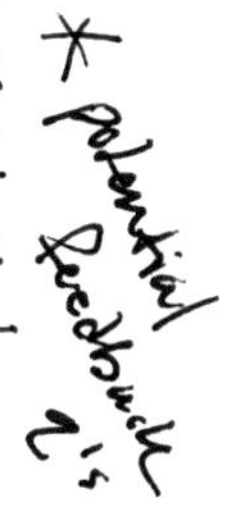

To Name Is Humility. To Ignore Is Dangerous.

If you shared with someone that you had a difficult decision to make, one of the earliest pieces of advice they'd offer is to seek the wisdom of others. Wisdom from the minds and experiences of others has its place, particularly within an abolitionist approach, because a part of our pursuit of freedom is based on partnering with our teaching and learning community to seek emancipation. However, we must discover the difference in seeking the wisdom of others as guidance, and allowing the lived experiences of others to become our choices. The grueling, complex suffering of having to make dangerous decisions for the sake of the community is part of the abolitionist approach. Dangerous decisions must be formed and informed by the human dysfunctions, trauma coping, procedural ambiguities, communication stress, inadequate information, inconsistent details, and role nuance particular to the teaching and learning community you are leading. Harriet Tubman and Sojourner Truth made distinct choices of how they used hymns and spirituals in their abolition against slavery. Both were spirited, resilient, and dangerous actors in the pursuit of freedom, but through choices that were responsive to their contexts. Truth employed hymns to disarm the hostility of whiteness, and Tubman as coded language for alerting the enslaved of the departure—and both were formed and informed by a set of irreplicable ambiguities. When there is clarity of values at the philosophical level of decision-making, these decisions are emancipated from the control of others *beyond* the teaching and learning community, and become those of the leader in partnership with the community.

Who was in the cockpit with Captain Sully? Officer Skiles. Who was on the plane with them? Three flight attendants and 150 passengers. One hundred and fifty-three people on Flight 1549, in community, reliant on the decisions of two leaders. And of those two, *only* one was leading their pursuit. It was a distinct, traumatic, ambiguous, hasty moment where the words of others in the comfort of a control tower were limited in scope and power to the intensity of being there. In *that* moment. Many had, in their minds, a seemingly rational notion that those in the tower had choices that Captain Sully should have pursued in the throes of that moment. The *Wall Street Journal* published a report of flight simulations in which pilots turned the plane around, successfully, and landed at LaGuardia Airport after losing power in both engines at the same point as Flight 1549. Even Patrick, a well-meaning air traffic controller, offered Captain Sully choices, the recurring of which was "to try to get us back to a runway at LaGuardia."[2] But there is a problem—a problem with those simulations, and a problem with Patrick. Those simulations were recreated, on the ground, from the safety of simulation labs; and Patrick was on the ground, in an air traffic control tower. Neither Patrick nor those simulation pilots were in *that* Airbus in the air, at 240 miles per hour, descending from 3,060 feet to 1,650 feet.

Barry Schiff, a retired pilot who has flown more than 300 different kinds of aircraft, didn't respond well to the notion of retrospective, simulation-flights. "What's the worst that can happen?" he says. "You reset the simulator and try it again."[3] Schiff alludes to the trauma of making choices in crisis moments. The mental and emotional state that a pilot experiences in an emergency cannot be compared to a simulated state. Much the same, as leaders of teaching and learning communities, we will inevitably find ourselves in heighted emotional and mental states, having to make decisions in the abolitionist interest of our students, staff, and families. It is inevitable. When our decisions are imminent, we are often advised and even compelled to pursue certain pathways by district leaders, city and state accountability boards, board of trustees and advisory councils, and accreditation teams. While mostly well-intentioned and commonly guided by prior experiences, there is a problem. Those folx are not in *our* community with *our* human dysfunctions, trauma coping, procedural ambiguities, communication stress, inadequate information, inconsistent details, and role nuance. That is the impetus of ignoring them. It is not regarded as disrespect or contempt for their charge to fulfill their roles. It is, instead, the highest regard for our communal consciousness. It is esteem for the pursuit of freedom. It is reverence for the lived experiences, knowledge, and traumas of those in the plane with us as leaders, descending at 240 miles per hour.

It is therefore necessary, as abolitionists, that teaching and learning leaders make intentional decisions to ignore the lived experiences of others from shadowing choices that disrupt freedom. The affective choice in ignoring, as an act of resistance, the sociocultural and sociopolitical powers that be is a dangerous one. Dangerous in that ignored powers tend to use defensive mechanisms, oppressive threats, and subjugating tactics to reify positional politics. These mechanisms, threats, and tactics can be at the expense of what is in the freedom interest of the students within the teaching and learning community. As an abolitionist, ignore anyway. The act of ignoring is not only dangerous, it is also dramatic. In its drama, it is staged—philosophically and strategically.

Avoid Breaking the Fourth Wall

Growing up in St. Louis, my mother was a patron of the largest professional Black theatre company in the nation—The Black Repertory, founded in 1976 by Ron Himes. We would attend every show, mostly on Saturday for the matinee, and it was the highlight of the weekend. Second only to church, the fashions and culture of Black excellence were on full display and pageantry as we arrived at The Grandel. It was a majestic, Romanesque Revival church built in 1884 with colossally cut limestone, patinated copper, and pristinely maintained stained glass. For a few summers, The Black Repertory would host an eight-week performing arts intensive, which is where I was introduced to acting, but no longer as the audience.

Stage sets are built with right, left, and back walls, referring to the *three* varying perspectives from the audience. But there is a fourth perspective, an imaginary "fourth" wall located at the front of the stage. As a performance convention, it is an invisible point of separation between the actors and the audience. Konstantin Stanislavski called it "public solitude,"[4] which is described as acting in public as if were you in private. Breaking the fourth wall occurs when the actors ignore this invisible wall and engage with the audience directly. "When you break the fourth wall," Ron used to tell us, "there is no repairing it—the audience now knows you can engage them, *and they can engage you. And* rarely does the audience know the rules governing how the stage behaves. You have to follow the rules."

As abolitionist teaching and learning leaders, we must create a fourth wall between the sociocultural and sociopolitical powers that be and ourselves, a wall that philosophically, strategically, and operationally draws a distinction between our actions and the audience of those powers. When you do the work of making dangerous decisions, it will compel you to ignore the noises, movements, sneers, and stoniness of those who are in the audience of your decision-making. In our teaching and learning communities, the role of district offices, accountability committees, charter authorization teams, and the like is to offer counsel, but as abolitionists we are free to decide whether to engage that counsel. This is not a hard and fast maxim that must be abided by. Actors and actresses break the fourth wall and engage with their audiences when the value of engagement outweighs the disruption of engagement. Much the same, when the value of engaging the powers that power be outweighs their disruption in our pursuit of freedom for all students, we break the wall. When do you break it? Consider three things.

Relationship. Breaking the fourth wall is an act, a choice about relationship—it forms and informs how a performer and audience exist in relationship to one another. When a performer engages the audience, there's an intimacy, a connection there. Ask yourself: does our school-based relationship with the powers that be—the district superintendent, local or state Board of Education, community educational council, charter authorizer, philanthropic foundation, or the independently governed Board of the school/network itself (in a public charter or Independent context)—indicate that they are co-conspirators in a collective pursuit of freedom for all students, namely Black students? Without a clear, co-conspirator relationship with the powers that be, you maintain an obligation as an abolitionist school leader to determine in moments of crisis if the fourth wall should be broken. At the moment you break the fourth wall to invite the powers that be to engage in pragmatic decision-making that impacts the overall communal consciousness of the school, you are held responsible for how that engagement impacts and influences the students and families within your care.

Disruption. If you pay close attention to the structure of performances with horror and psychological thrill, breaking the wall is a mechanism to disrupt the expectations of the audience. It unnerves and rattles the audience by forcing it to directly interact with the performer, oblivious to what might happen, or what might be said. Ask yourself: how will you act in ways to disrupt the powers that be, forcing them to come frontal with your abolitionist ideals? As an abolitionist, you maintain the authority to disrupt, unnerve, and rattle power by the ways you decide to act. In crises of all kinds impacting real human lives, powers like district leaders and charter oversight boards have been known to take risk-adverse positions, uneasy with rattling the status quo.

Think about the memos intended to provide guidance and strategic recommendations that we have received in fiscal crisis or political disaster. Rarely, and I do mean *rarely,* do they ever offer guidance that has communal freedom and the emancipation of students and families at the core. Rarely, and I do mean *rarely,* do powers that be recommend courses of action that prioritize the oppressed and dejected. Thus, I have discovered during my time in leadership that breaking the fourth wall as an act of disrupting the powers that be has required me, more times than not, to answer the age-old question: *do what is expedient, or do what is right?* As an abolitionist, the answer is clear. We have an obligation to disrupt and rattle their status quo by acting in ways that are right for our students and families, forcing the powers that be to come face-to-face with our abolitionist rhythms.

Teaching. When a performer is preparing to enter into a complex subject with detailed material, she dramatically breaks the fourth wall as a tactical teaching method. It is to offer the audience the necessary details to hold the coming moment with clarity and understanding. Ask yourself: are we in a strategic position to be a trusted teaching source for the powers that be in how we choose to act in *this* moment? Never forget that above all, you are still a teacher. It is easy to become so consumed with our offices, meeting schedules, budget protocols, compliance audits, Board preparation, and grievance fielding that we forget that we are still teachers. And as teachers, we must create moments in crisis to teach, thus causing the powers that be to learn. Abolitionists of yesterdays, like Douglass and Truth, often had to act in ways that became lessons for white folx, those who aspired to be abolitionist and those who were securely oppressors. These lessons oft-yielded new ways of thinking birthed out of lived experiences and knowledge that would be foreign to the learner. As such, often times our actions in moments of crisis are lessons for folx in power, particularly white folx in power, because Black and brown and oppressed actions are often the direct result of lived experiences and knowledge. Should we *have* to teach those in power? No. But should we ever abdicate our role as teachers? No.

Acting as a Group

What is the difference between a crowd of random individuals boarding the Six Line on the MTA Subway in New York City and a group of teachers marching down Fifth Avenue in protest of reopening school buildings amidst a global pandemic? What is the difference between a group of oncology researchers pursuing a cure for breast cancer in isolated labs all over the world and a group of oncology researchers collaborating to discover the long-term impact of gene-replacement on cancer patients? What about the difference between 230 information technology professionals all over a university system working to resolve a potential network outage in their department, and the entire information technology team working in tandem to advance a network update without disruptions for the entire system? The intuitive answer is no secret. *Acting as a group*. Group actions have clear, communal aims, which demand a level of optimized priority, collective intention, clarity of role, and strategic pursuits on the parts of the participants toward each other and toward the aim itself. In an abolitionist context, a group is more than the sum total of the individuals. A group is the collective embodiment of a pursuit that impacts the advancement or postponement of a communal consciousness. In practice, the folx within the group regard themselves and each other as co-conspirators in a pursuit—a pursuit that they embrace by individually knowing how they fit, while acting out of and within consideration of the communal aim.

As abolitionist as it might be, I must confess that acting as a group with optimized priority, collective intention, and clarity of role is arduous, on both human and organizational levels. Why? Because in the pursuit of freedom, *how* to get there and *who* does what on the way, there is often a struggle of minds and wills. So, what does a group of highly experienced, well-degreed, abolitionist-aspiring leaders do after ten months of digital instruction as the coming academic year approaches? What does a group do in the freedom interest of students and families and staff when there are varying perspectives on what looks, feels, and sounds the right thing to do? *It acts.* To start, the group acts by making a series of agreements—often philosophical and broadly interpreted—that become the humanizing and centralizing strategic priorities that ground and guide the group through every decision.

In March 2020, as Covid-19 was growing in New York City, and our organization made the critical decision, weeks ahead of the Department of Education to transition to fully virtual instruction, we had to make a series of urgent group-supported decisions that would impact thousands of folx, from students to families to staff. Spending hours upon hours upon hours with principals, network leaders, and senior leaders, it was clear that the impact of Covid-19 would be widespread, ranging from teaching to budgeting; and therefore, our agreements to meet the needs of our students, staff, teachers, leaders, social workers, families, and support staff would have to be agreements that any member of the group can connect with when those moments of tension and storming grow in decision-making. We learned early in the crisis, around April, that our city and state, both of which thrived on the revenue from sales tax, would be adversely impacted and that impact would be felt by every industry that directly serves people, from education to healthcare to transportation to social services. But we also learned early that the impact wouldn't be felt immediately, but would demand an uncanny patience as we awaited the governor's and the mayor's decisions around budgeting. In our waiting, as leaders from across our organization, we committed as a group to following principles, each of which would guide our own decisions and the decisions of our teams as we waded the crisis.

- we will deliver the mission of our organization
- we will uphold and embody our core values
- we will value, support, and protect the interests of our students
- we will preserve our investments in inclusive teaching, learning, and care
- we will make short-term adjustments to sustain the organization long-term
- we will stress test our priorities by doing more with less

- we will communicate vulnerably and transparently in our decisions
- we will prioritize science by maximizing the safety of our staff and community

With more than 2,400 students across all our schools and programs, more than 1,100 families, and more than 300 employees, we made decisions rapidly from March until August, each of which was responsive to new information from national, state, and local sources. In the rising thick of a national crisis, as a group, we didn't have weeks and months to deliberate, weigh our options, evaluate the pros and cons, develop hierarchal chains of decision-making, and wait for guidance from district and state and city officials on how best to serve our schools. We often had days, sometimes hours. As unemployment grew in our community, service jobs ceased, social service agencies closed down, grocery stores (in what is already a food apartheid) limited hours and access to fresh produce, we had to act. Our city's Department of Education and many other networks of schools and education-adjacent organizations defaulted to white cultural norms of conversations for conversation-sake, either/or thinking, memo after memo, power hoarding, and the perpetuation of individualism.[5] We did the opposite. We rejected white supremacy culture by humanizing, flattening, and streamlining our actions as a group by remaining grounded and guided by our principles.

One of our deputy superintendents, who was transitioning from being a principal for six years, said:

> Principals need the freedom to act, and their actions must be aligned. If their actions aren't aligned, families will be confused, staff will be confused, because you know they talk, and we can't risk that. As long as we know from you [meaning me, as superintendent] the direction we're going in and how much risk we can take without

> approval, then we know how much risk we can allow teachers to take. And if we know that, we'll get it done. They'll get it done. It'll get done.

It was all hands on deck, and all of the groups within our organization rose to the challenge because we had collective intention, clarity of roles, and optimized priorities in the form of our guiding principles. With that level of alignment, everyone in the community is acting. Even if folx are seemingly doing nothing, their doing nothing is acting. That is why no action is in isolation of another action, even if we cling to that faulty assumption.

In our case, all of our leaders knew that when you lose days, weeks, and months to act, for the sake of the community, *not acting* is not an option. And what is core to acting as a group is establishing the communal norm that often our group actions will compel us to focus less on actions as functions of a title, and actions as functions of strengths. Our deputy superintendent emphasizes this norm in sharing that "we'll get it done. They'll get it done. It'll get done." Why? Because acting as a group, effectively, is about getting it done within the context of a communal pursuit, without respect of person. Imagine if our school leaders had to wait for me to make every decision and, then, imagine if I had to wait for our Board to approve every decision that school leaders wanted to make. Power hoarding, as a practice, is in direct opposition of creating an abolitionist rhythm because acting *well* is not about individual power and individual values for the sake of egoism. Contrariwise, acting *well* is about ensuring that each distinctive contribution—the strengths within the community—and distinctive values—the dignity within the community—is understood and known as being part of the larger pursuit. When contributions and values are outside of an understanding of the larger pursuit, and exist beyond the agreed-upon principles that ground and guide that pursuit, the acts within teaching and learning communities will inherently be entangled in a power politics that prohibits freedom. The notion of individual strengths and individual values does not discount the role of titles and positions within a teaching and learning community. But it contextualizes titles and positions by reimagining and reframing their function in communities as shared responsibility—each with value to the whole, not as a concentration and hoarding of power. Experiencing titles and positions as shared responsibility, each person within the community, particularly in times of crisis, can situate their contributions as meaningful, indispensable, and liberatory.

I must confess that as we navigated the nuanced, principle-informed terrain of acting as a group, there were primarily two barriers to our approach. One barrier was that we have been so socialized and shaped by hierarchy that we often look for it even when we request autonomy. The other is that while we had principles, which guided our decision-making, workstreams crossed multiple folx and lanes, which periodically delayed decision-making because of the nuance of where decisions rested. In retrospect, a decision tree would have prevented the bottlenecking of many of our decisions. A decision tree is a branched flowchart, which illustrates multiple pathways for potential decisions, the potential outcomes flowing from each decision, and the decision makers at each interval of the decision, which would have clarified lanes and workstreams. Using a tool like a decision tree would have emancipated groups from the grip of hierarchy, which would have resulted in groups acting more effectively and efficiently.

Though it wasn't explicitly named, Flight 1549 had a clear decision tree as it navigated crisis. Imagine the outcome if the flight attendants would have called, "Mayday Mayday Mayday." Without the view of the pilot and a pilot's understanding of the plane, the flight attendants acting as a group would have compounded a crisis by functioning outside of their lane. Instead, Captain Sully—operating in his workstream—called, "Mayday, Mayday, Mayday," while flight attendants began telling passengers to close tray tables, bring seats upright, lower their heads, and brace for impact. By operating in distinct lanes (latent with hierarchy, yes, but not restrictively)—one group acting out of warning (the pilots) and the other group acting out of orderliness (the attendants)—human life was safeguarded.

Almost a month to the day after the dramatic incident, on February 16, 2009, a writer for *Air & Space* spoke with Captain Sully who underscored the mutuality of each role within a community while acting as a group. Here's their conversation.

INTERVIEWER: I heard you say in one of your interviews that it was comforting to you to hear the flight attendants, after you announced "Brace for impact," also directing the passengers to brace and put their heads down. Why was that a source of comfort?

CAPTAIN SULLY: I felt they were assisting me in that moment. Even though we were intensely focused and very busy, I remember thinking that as soon as I made the public address announcement in the cabin, within a second or two, I heard even through the hardened cockpit door the flight attendants in unison shouting their commands. "Heads down. Stay down." And it was comforting to me to know that they were on the same page, that we were all acting in concert. It made me feel that my hope and my confidence in completing this plan was reasonable and that they knew what needed to be done and were doing their part.

When freedom is the pursuit, acting as a group is the strategy. At the intersection of three crises—health, economic, and racial—all of our teaching and learning communities were distressed for most of 2020, and into 2021, and our burden was, and remains, to lead them toward a free, and more just place. Largely unnoticed and immensely undervalued during these times is the task of cooperative and interdependent acting, where every individual in that pursuit of a freer and just place understands his or her contribution and value. Any assumption that a teaching and learning community can achieve freedom for the oppressed by the actions of one is a reflection of frailty. Of the many rejected *isms* of abolition, acting as a group rejects *individualism*.

You Can't Act on Everything at Once

As school leaders, we know—or, we should know—that even the smallest glitch during a time of heightened communal consciousness can have critical impact, so we have to center keeping folx focused on acting in the freedom interest of students. Why? Because in a crisis, everything functions like a critical priority, whether it's a real or perceived priority. But even with everything as a priority, we were clear at the early peak of the pandemic, and the ongoing racial unrest that we had three main strategic priorities: (1) *continuous teaching, learning, community, and care for all students*, (2) *holding intentional space for our teachers and staff to be well*, and (3) *operating leanly by alleviating all expenses misaligned with the first and second goals*. As the fall approached, and we braced for a second wave of Covid-19 cases with reopening schools ahead of heard immunity or a vaccine, the temptation grew to make everything a critical priority. But we deepened our commitment to the initial three priorities, and added a fourth priority—*deepening and advancing our use of technology*. Why? Because the more we leaned into the initial three priorities, and the longer we operationalized our reopening of schools, the clearer it became that technology was going to be essential to actualizing those priorities in just, equitable, and freeing ways for all students, and particularly for our economically-vulnerable students. We had to act, but we couldn't act on everything at once. We had to choose. And the only way to choose is to imagine, categorize, and evaluate our choices. Before a performer knows what she is going to do, before Captain Sully knew how we was going to land Flight 1549, before we knew how we were going to construct a new normal of teaching and learning post-Covid-19, and before you know how you are going to lead your teaching and learning community to freedom, it starts with using an imagination of evaluation.

We all know that we can't act on everything at once. But do we *really know* that we can't act on everything at once? In a society of competing priorities and conflicting philosophies, being clear on what you are going to prioritize has less to do with an interminable scientific process, nor is there anything magical about it. It has everything to do with evaluating the priorities transparently and realistically, evaluating them against an abolitionist framework of freedom, and evaluating them in relationship to the risks of *not acting*, and the impact of those risks on the most oppressed folx within our community. But the risks of not acting are not the only evaluation criteria to weigh varying priorities. For us, the evaluation criteria centered on prioritizing choices that reduced disruption to our students and families, disproportionately Black and brown and economically-vulnerable, as much as humanly possible; and for Captain Sully, the evaluation criteria were about saving lives at the loss of the plane. As abolitionists, our rhythms are the criteria by which to weigh the choices and priorities before us. Against the operational evaluation criteria—time, cost, human capital, and feasibility—Sully had clear philosophical criteria that informed the evaluation process, and so did we. But there's a catch. All criteria are not created equal.

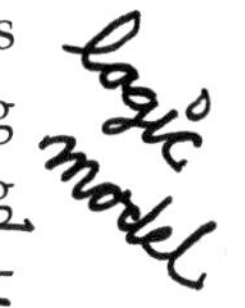

In conventional leadership, the operational evaluation criteria would be weighed as having the most influence. That is not the case in crisis, nor is it the case when we are advancing a communal consciousness of freedom and justice in our teaching and learning communities. For us, what has the most influence is the choice, or priority, which is the closest to the level of beginning the emancipation process. The farther away the choices and priorities are from emancipation, the farther they should be away from the consciousness of the abolitionist leaders—delegate those distant-from-freedom choices to others within the community. Why delegate? Evaluating the prioritization of choices is an exhaustible resource, and when a leader is obligated, *by intention or by refusal to delegate*, to evaluate them all, it will inevitably lead to analysis paralysis. As an abolitionist, ask—what does this priority, or choice, have to say about the freedom of all oppressed folx? If the priority or choice is misaligned to abolitionist pursuits, or is an obstruction to freedom, then weigh that priority or choice as one that does not demand your commitment. If the priority or choice is compelling in the pursuit of freedom, but demands reimagining our strategic and operational tactics as abolitionist because they have not been reimagined yet, then weigh that priority as viable for commitment. But if the priority or choice is compelling in the pursuit of freedom, and it aligns with our abolitionist strategic and operational tactics, then weigh that priority as *the one* for commitment. Optimizing one philosophical, strategic, and operational alignment in our weighing of criteria leads us to *the priority.* Not all of the priorities, but *the priority.* We optimized equitable non-disruption. Sully optimized human life. At all costs, abolition optimizes freedom.

It's an Act of Commitment

The virtue of the notion of optimizing alignment to identify *the priority* amidst many priorities is that by identifying *the priority,* we are living out where we stand and must commit to standing there. Identifying the priority is an act of commitment. It is an act of standing confidently. And note that standing where you stand with confidence is not an incongruity with humility. In fact, standing where you stand on a priority, confidently, should be an indicator that you have done the task of humility by naming the problem and evaluating the priorities, and have arrived where you have arrived with what Søren Kierkegaard calls "fear and trembling." Foundational to the Hebrew bible and the Judeo-Christian tradition is Abraham, known in the tradition as "Father Abraham" because he is considered one of the patriarchs of faith. Over the centuries, Abraham has become quintessential for *committing* to acts of unwavering resolve, because he is most storied in his willingness to sacrifice—which should be read ethically as "kill"—his son Isaac as a commitment of what he identified as a priority in devotion to the divine. In the narrative, Abraham is ordered by the divine, as an optimization of prioritzing his resolute faith to kill his son. As he is preparing to commit the act, the divine intervenes and offers an alternative in the form of a ram for him. Ultimately, it was his unwavering resolve to follow-through with an inconceivable act that ensured the future of his posterity. Kierkegaard, a Danish philosopher and theologian, explores how Abraham recognizes that our decisions, choices, and priorities cannot always be justified in sociocultural and sociopolitical contexts. The notion that Abraham would be so committed to a priority—devotion to the divine—that he would be willing to kill his son Isaac, which sociocultural context would deem ineffable, is evidence that Abraham recognizes that committing to a choice is about duty to something higher. As abolitionists, our higher duty is freedom. But we have potentially misread the intent of the narrative. What if, in fact, the narrative of Abraham is less about his willingness to commit the act, and more about the fear and trembling induced as a result of committing to an act? What if the core of Abraham's unwavering resolve is a coming to terms with the inherent fear within our commitments to higher duties like freedom, justice, and emancipation? As humans in pursuit of freedom, when everything is a priority and every priority is a choice, we must choose *the priority* of freedom—and then have an Abrahamic *commitment*. A commitment that can be maintained in the face of fear and in the shadow of doubt, because that commitment transcends our human understanding. It's a passionately human, but no less divine commitment. It's not an eternal commitment, but it is an ethereal commitment, full of as much possibility and opportunity as it is full of fear and trembling. And, because of its possibility and opportunity, we must stand on it.

How do you know where you stand? Begin with simple record keeping. List all of the difficult decisions you can recall—*all of them*. Consider what made the decision complicated and what philosophical truths, if any, you had to stand on to reach the choice you did for the community you were leading. Consider the fear and trembling, the worry and doubt, the anxiety and anticipation that was associated with each choice you've made. Once you've organized your history of decisions, and judiciously analyzed those decisions against an abolitionist framework of freedom, you should be able to see patterns and rhythms for where you have stood in times past. And then, look within. Deep within. Abolitionist leaders are willing to look inward, ahead of pursuing any pathway with the community, and examine themselves. For often, our past performance in moments of crisis and reckoning are guiding, but not fixed, indicators of where we tend to stand. Of course, abolition invites opportunities for reinvention, so our past precedents should be not evaluted as fixed guidance for future action. Yet, they cannot be ignored. But I must warn you—pattern recognition can distort decision-making, which is why it must not exist in isolation of soul searching. What is soul searching in decision-making? In this abolitionist leadership context, it is probing one's self to identify decisions that sing a new song of freedom within, songs that are as passionately human and radically moral as they are divine in pursuing a universal freedom for all folx. In an attempt to recreate, and continue the pattern of the past, often from a place of decision-making comfort, we run the risk of ignoring the distinguishing details of *this moment*, and the interpretive nuance of each crisis and decision-making moment within our souls, thus interfering with our reflective capacity to act in a moment *for the moment*.

Eavesdropping on a conversation at Kroger, the largest supermarket retailer in the United States, on Farmington Boulevard in Germantown, Tennessee, a woman admonished her wife, "Don't allow misleading memories to make you repeat a mistake. You know you have a tendency to overvalue your memories in tough decisions." Many of us are as her wife. We, too, have a tendency to overvalue the patterns within our memories of what we have done and how we have done it, when we are in an unclear decision-making moment. To mitigate, or reduce, this risk in determining where we stand today, we must inquire of ourselves—

1. When I stood where I stood, what was specific to that moment about why I stood there? And what new information, value system, or relationship has emerged that forms and informs where I stand now? Is where I stand on this issue, or is the choice I am preparing to make, in alignment with the abolitionist rhythms I've committed to? Or, is where I stand and the choice I am preparing to make a reifying of oppression and injustice?
2. What patterns, evidences, or indicators of standing where I have stood in the history of leading this teaching and learning community were formed and informed by patterns I observed in others, evidences that were under- and/or over-privileged, or indicators that were beyond my control? Are the patterns I've observed real or perceived, and how do those patterns reveal the ways I navigate fear and trembling in making abolitionist decisions?
3. What barriers exist, what barriers have I created, or what barriers are inherent to this teaching and learning community that stand in the way of me standing where I want to stand on this issue? How do I partner to alleviate the barriers present in order to make a choice that stands in a place on an issue that speaks to my soul?
4. Who can I consult from when I stood where I stood in order to conduct a distortion-check of whether I recall standing where I stood with accuracy? And, who can I ask to be an accountability partner for where I want to stand moving forward in making choices on freedom, justice, and emancipation?

Utilizing aforementioned soul-searching questions positions you to get clearer on where you stand as an abolitionist actor in decision-making; and by knowing where you stand, you position yourself to *commit, commit, commit* when you have evaluated choices and determined the one that affirms an abolitionist ethic of freedom. How is it that enslaved Black women, men, and families were able to commit on where they stood in pursuing escape? The answer is that they had weighed, heard, seen, and potentially even experienced the risk of not committing. Not committing increased the risks of being captured and returned. Not committing increased the risks of bodily oppression. This was, at least on the surface, part of what reifies one's commitment to the pursuit—because the possibilities of committing to freedom outweigh the risks of not committing. We must keep the same calculation.

Acting as Being

Think for a moment about what the story of Captain Sully teaches us. It teaches us that our notion of what it means to act—and to act *dangerously*—particularly in crisis, is too simplified when we make acting about what we do. Yes, acting is doing. But acting is being. Captain Sully knew how to act dangerously because he embodied an ethic of acting in the interest of humanity. At 3:27:11pm, when those Canadian geese were sucked into the engine turbines, he did not have to choose to act, because he embodied acting. And that is the definitive danger of acting. It is an embodiment. When we experience our acts of resistance as part of who we are, as humans, not as what we do as leaders, then our pursuit is never cheapened to its function. It is valued for its being. Abrahamic commitment, as an abolitionist ideal, is not about what he *did* in committing. It is about *who* he was in committing. Abrahamic abolitionism—a concept worth more exploration beyond this book—, then, is when prioritizing acting is an extension of your humanity as being, and the *choices* that extend from your humanity in the world are testaments of one's inherent being. In effect, Abraham was prepared to act with unwavering resolve not as an act for act's sake, but as an act for being's sake.

From the 1800s through the early twentieth century through the Jim Crow era through the HIV/AIDS crisis to modern voter suppression and the social media-exposed rise of white supremacy, the pursuit of freedom has been advanced by the communal consciousness of abolitionists who, by fear and trembling, embodied the pursuit of freedom at the risk of resentment. It is not a moment. It is an existence. It is not an act. It is an identity. And today, at a time when teaching and learning communities are experiencing a new wave of calls for abolitionism through community protests and national reckoning, the advancement of freedom is not about producing. It is about being.

Notes

1. On January 15, 2019, the tenth anniversary of Flight 1549, Captain Chesley "Sully" Sullenberger tweeted a live recollection of the events that took place.
2. Pasztor, Andy. (May 4, 2010). "'Hudson Miracle' gets closer look." *The Wall Street Journal*. Retrieved from https://www.wsj.com/articles/SB10001424052748703612804575222482042335978.
3. Paur, Jason. (May 5, 2010). "Sullenberger made the right move, landing in the Hudson." *Wired*. Retrieved from https://www.wired.com/2010/05/ntsb-makes-recommendations-after-miracle-on-the-hudson-investigation/.
4. Hinckley, Jaren S. (2008). "Performance anxiety: Constantin Stanislavski's concept of public solitude." *College Music Symposium*, Vol. 48, 124.
5. Jones, Kenneth & Okun, Tema. (2001). "White Supremacy Culture." In *Dismantling Racism: A Resource Book for Social Change Groups*. Portland, OR: Western States Center, 49.

6

Just Say the Thing: Communicating Clearly, Directly, and Humanely

What do we say? Who says it, and does it matter who says it? Who do we say it to? How do we say it? Are we saying too much? Are we saying enough? Will our community misinterpret what we're saying? Are we misinterpreting what we are saying? Who might be offended by what we say? Do we care about offending? Do we put it in writing, host an in-person or virtual town hall, send a pre-recorded message, or all of those? What day and time do we send it? Is anything else being said that day? Do we say something twice, or thrice? Should the Board see it first? How many drafts do we need? Have we controlled for our language biases? Do you have a student version, teacher version, and family version? Can we have a universal version for everyone? Should it go to the press? What if the press gets ahold of it without our consent? What are we forgetting?

Whether you're leading a classroom through a challenging conversation of gender identity after careless words surfaced in the bathroom, or you're leading a school through a restorative process after the murder of a student through senseless gun-violence, or you're leading a network of schools through reopening its buildings and campuses amidst a devastating, life-altering pandemic, it is simply impossible to be effective in any of those crises without being an effective communicator. When teaching and learning delivery is disrupted, and students and teachers inquire about the impact it has on them, and the larger community, effective communication is prime; because, no matter how much you believe that students, teachers, and families trust your credibility and ethicality in pursuit of freedom and justice, it can all be invalidated within seconds on the part of ineffective and/or oppressive communication.

Many leaders have the physiological capacity of speech; but effective leaders have the cultivated and practiced skill of communication. "Being a great communicator does not mean being a great talker. There is a big difference between the two, the thrust of gaining more knowledge separates excellent communicator from a good talker."[1] Within our abolitionist approach, let's define communication as a means of exchanging meaningful, influential, and intentional knowledge for the freedom sake of the community receiving the knowledge. Freedom, in this sense, could be freedom to trust leadership, freedom to assuage anxiety, freedom to make decisions, or most deeply, freedom to hope. Contrary to what many of us were led to believe, or even taught—intentionally or unintentionally—the most imperative principles of effective communication as an abolitionist communicator are not exclusive to outlining, number of drafts, reviews, and paragraphic protocols. Important? Yes. Meaningful? Sure. *Imperative? No.* An effective, abolitionist communicator has an ability to take seriously and center the more subtle, humane, and humanizing principles of communication—principles rarely taught in the classroom, because they are other-focusing, other-enhancing, and other-centering. These rarely taught, and even less practiced principles are tone, level of ambiguity, identifiable outcomes, agitation effect, and balancing passionately human, radically moral compassion with fact-based knowledge.

Put yourself at Corinthian Hall in Rochester, New York on July 5, 1852 when Frederick Douglass posed a question that continues to reverberate in the very soul of America: "What, to the American slave, is your 4th of July?" When we think of Douglass, one of the preeminent thoughts that come to mind is his ability to effectively and emotively communicate by balancing factual claims against the democratic injustice of America with the humane conviction of imagining a moral reconstruction—a balancing act of communication quite distinct from the ability to talk. Douglas, humbly and evocatively, decenters himself, as a freed Black man, in service of the project of communicating the communal consciousness of enslaved Black folx.

> I shall see, this day, and its popular characteristics, from the slave's point of view. Standing, there, identified with the American bondman, making his wrongs mine, I do not hesitate to declare, with all my soul, that the character and conduct of this nation never looked blacker to me than on this 4th of July! Whether we turn to the declarations of the past, or to the professions of the present, the conduct of the nation seems equally hideous and revolting. America is false to the past, false to the present, and solemnly binds herself to be false to the future. Standing with God and the crushed and bleeding slave on this occasion, I will, in the name of humanity which is outraged, in the name of liberty which is fettered, in the name of the constitution and the Bible, which are disregarded and trampled upon, dare to call in question and to denounce, with all the emphasis I can command, everything that serves to perpetuate slavery—the great sin and shame of America! "I will not equivocate; I will not excuse"; I will use the severest language I can command; and yet not one word shall escape me that any man, whose judgment is not blinded by prejudice, or who is not at heart a slaveholder, shall not confess to be right and just.[2]

Underpinning every scathing sentiment of Douglass' critique of the moral crisis defining the American project was a provocative, human, humane, and imaginative conviction that offered a vulnerable boldness unforgettable to the listener. "Abolitionists were not just quintessential agitators but also wordsmiths. Whatever they lacked in power, they made up for by outproducing their mighty opponents in [communication] …"[3] One of the misconceptions of communicating through crises is that, as leaders, our words must continuously inspire, oft doubly misconceived as meaning that we must instill positivity. Abolition isn't positive; abolition is agitation. Crises aren't positive; crises are provocative. As such, Douglass offers us an understanding of communicating through moral crises that has less to do with inspiration in a classical sense of creating joy, and more to do with inspiration in a convictional sense of creating agitation that leads to freedom. Abolitionist communication is about creating an intersectional moment where the mind (facts), the emotion (humanity), and the soul (conviction) have a mutual understanding of why the crisis exists, how the crisis impacts and oppresses the community, where the community should situate itself in relationship to the crisis, and what the emancipating actions will be. Consequently, we will position ourselves as abolitionist leaders to secure indispensable trust, necessary for the sustainability and the stress of the freedom work.

Managing the tenor of a teaching and learning community, establishing trust in pursuit of freedom, and laying the necessary foundation to act decisively and boldly with the community demands a leader who is willing to risk perfection for the sake of abolition. Communicating amidst, or immediately after, a crisis is unlike any other form of communication because you are holding in tension the intersection of fact-based information and radically human compassion; as such, perfection is often the enemy of an abolitionist communicator, in that perfection will delay what the community is anxious to know. Any leader committed to the pursuit of freedom within their teaching and learning community must be equally and ethically committed to alleviating the aura of anxiety, in that anxiety has the capacity to impede trust, and any imposition to trust will impede progress.

The Directness Principle

Raised in a Black matriarchal household, I quickly discovered the *directness principle*. One of the ways my mother built my resilience, as her only Black male child, for the white world through which I'd have to navigate was in the practice of directness, often colloquially described as "say what you mean, and mean what you say." Oddly, though, that directness was never utilized to communicate callously and heartlessly. On the contrary, directness was a form of humane communication that removed any illusory barriers between those communicating. The path to abolitionist communication requires the directness principle for the sake of the community. We must start, again, by asking, how does a lack of directness oppress Black folx and other marginalized identities? By doing exactly what my mother set out *not to do* in communicating with me—creating illusory truths. When leaders fail to be direct in our communication, particularly when we are leading teaching and learning communities that disproportionately serve Black folx, brown folx, and income insecure folx, we suppress freedom. The nuance and complexity of directness are that, in approach, it can be perceived as merciless; and yet, it is the epitome of mercy in that directness takes seriously that knowing what a thing is, how a thing is going to be, and the impact a thing will have offers folx a freedom to plan, prepare, and position themselves according to the outcomes that make most sense for their households and lived experiences. In a way, a lack of directness on the part of leaders has an air of individualism and selfishness by withholding meaningful, influential, and intentional knowledge from the community. The point here is that the directness principle nippily alleviates any imagined, perceived, or actual internal fears and concerns in the recipient of the knowledge, and gives the recipient clarity on what is to come.

Anyone who has ever worked with me has inevitably, and perhaps nauseatingly, heard my four-word rule for the directness principle—*just say the thing*. It is seemingly a simple act, yet it is loaded with complexity and anxiety and wonderings and questions and reluctance by so many. I often wonder if our reluctance to just saying the thing is, in part, because we lack clarity on what *the thing* is. Think about it: one can't say something if one doesn't know what one is saying; and being able to know *the thing*, not all the things, is a revolutionary act of directness. The problem is seldom that leaders don't know *things* to say, but that they regularly lack knowledge of *the thing*. As someone who values the potency of language, English has two article types—definite (the) and indefinite (a/an). As you might remember from elementary and middle school grammar lessons, *the* is used to refer to specific, particular, unambiguous nouns, while a/an is used for non-specific, non-particular, ambiguous nouns. So, the directness principle of just saying "*the* thing" is a principle first driven by a sense of discernment and sensitivity to a crisis, or a moment, in order to determine with unambiguous clarity *the thing* you are communicating.

As our senior management team contemplated how to communicate about the impending city and state budget cuts that would impact all New York City and State public schools, we went round after round about how much to say and how little to say, how many *other* things to say alongside *the thing* we really wanted to say; and after a few rounds of what could be interpreted by some as an incessant back-and-forth, I was asked why I was being so quiet, which was unlike me, and if I had any input on what we should do. By way of my mother's spirit, and in acknowledgment of what we risked by not employing *directness* as our driving principle, I replied,

> Just say the thing. Here is what's happening—cuts toward education, and other social impact areas, are on the table

> to rectify the budget gaps as a result of state and city revenue losses from Covid-19. We are unclear, at this point, of what those cuts might be. But what we do know is that they will range from 5% to 10%, potentially even more, by the end of the fiscal year. We have reviewed our budget, prioritized human capital, and made necessary adjustments to circumvent layoffs for as long as possible. We will be continually guided by the following principles—*x, y, and z*—and we will keep you informed, to the best of our ability, as we continue to learn more. *Just say the thing.*

The options for what we could have shared were endless, and there were a host of things being considered as additives for our communication to staff. Were the additives *things* that mattered? Potentially, to the folx who are always intrigued by more information than less. Were the additives *the thing*? No, and therefore, they flunked the directness test. In just saying *the thing*, we employ an abolitionist communication approach that accomplishes *five aims*: provides meaningful, influential, and intentional knowledge for the freedom sake of the community; affirms the impact of a crisis on *our* communal consciousness; rejects self-centered inclinations on the part of the leader by not centering how emotionally difficult it is to say, and instead focusing on what needs to be said; humanizes the lived experiences of the recipients as being deeply impacted by whatever is being communicated; and is steadfast in its pursuit, and sustaining, of freedom. Effectively executed, the directness principle points communication toward hope.

White leaders, however, must be mindful that the nature of systemic racism, positional power politics, and implicit biases adds a layer onto using the directness principle. This is because the historical trauma of directness rhetoric from white folx to oppressed folx, namely Black folx, has often resulted in bodily violence and psychological harm. *One way*, but certainly not the only way, to control for an abolitionist approach to the directness principle as a white leader is to oppression-test your communication by asking three guiding questions:

1. Am I the appropriate person to be talking about this issue? When I talk about this issue, what is the historical legacy of the issue itself and the words I'm going to use, and the historical consequences for oppressed folx in response to the issue I am going to address?
2. If someone read my spoken words without context of the situation, relationship with me personally or professionally, or without knowledge of the teaching and learning community I lead, how would they perceive the effect of my words on oppressed identities?
3. Who in my sphere of influence can I trust to hear, or read, my words and hold me accountable through a critical feedback-loop that intentionally checks my trivialization of traumas and identity politics, use of white-dominant norms, and/or my use of language that reinforces a deficit-based framing of non-white, non-privileged, non-hegemonic identities?

As a white leader, it's important to be honest with yourself that your use of the directness principle must be vetted, then vetted again, and then again in order to avoid perpetuating oppressive communication politics that calcifies existing narratives surrounding oppressed folx that are implicitly and explicitly harmful to the task of abolition. Further, oppressive messages in the smog of white privilege framing might be unintentional, and yet even unintentional harm must be identified and critiqued *directly*.

Framing—It's Not Just about What You Say, But *How*

In all communication, but particularly in abolitionist and justice-oriented communication where Black and oppressed folx are at risk, *framing* is everything. Robert Entman, one of the leading thinkers on framing, defines it as "the selection and highlighting, and use of the highlighted elements to construct an argument about problems and their causation, evaluation, and/or solution."[4] What reads as a simple concept influences and determines how *all of us* hear and read and receive information. Think about the role of varying news networks that represent polar differences in political ideology, like Fox News and MSNBC—framing is everything. The same story, framed by the ideological argument that each network is attempting to make, results in colossally distinct narratives about the cause of what is being covered, the evaluation of how the topic being covered impacts discourse, and effectively, how we as conspirators in democracy should respond to the topic. One of the longest framing arguments is the Israel/Palestine conflict, where two interpretive frames of history and legacy continue to inform every sociopolitical and sociocultural ideological debate that occurs in our two, dominate parties. Why? There is no agreed-upon framing of the conflict.

Framing happens whether we acknowledge it or not; and you might feel inclined to think of framing as merely point of view. More than point of view, however, framing has an intentional task to accomplish, which is to control and drive a particular narrative in order to mediate meaning-making between the one communicating and those listening. As Entman points out, framing is meant, "to promote a particular problem definition, causal interpretation, *moral evaluation*, and/or treatment recommendation ..."[5] Key to Entman's proposition is the "moral evaluation" being made about the topic being framed. As with all communication, our moral evaluation as part of our framing approach can be used as either an abolitionist tool in pursuit of freedom and justice and equity, or an oppressive tool in pursuit of false narratives and inferior identity politics and perpetual enslavement. At the basis of all framing in an abolitionist framework is the driving aim of freedom.

Against that backdrop, school leaders with an aspiration to be abolitionist communicators must utilize the driving frame of *freedom*. Why freedom? At our most human level, all of us are in pursuit of being free—free to our best selves, free to our truths, free to our identities, and free to our callings in the world. The American ideal of freedom, though *only* an actualized ideal for so few, is deeply imbedded in our communal consciousness as a nation and is central to the story of every identity in this country. And, from an abolitionist communication approach, freedom as the framing for building and executing an argument about problems and their causation, evaluation, and/or solution is directly tied to a moral evaluation of justice. There is, of course, a tension embedded with freedom as our framing. In a national climate where ideological politics has formed and informed how varying folx utilizes value words, freedom means different things to different people. When conservatives and progressives, to use a simple sociopolitical ideological binary, speak of freedom, hauntingly different frames are employed, leading communities to different understandings. That said, freedom, beyond political ideology, and captured in the deepest abolitionist sense, is the experience where "slavery and prejudice, sin and sorrow in every form [individual and institutional], are unfelt and unknown."[6]

An Abolitionist Communication Framework

As teaching and learning leaders do the work of framing communally conscious communication in the lens of freedom, be clear—it is a complex and weighty undertaking because human lives are on the line. With freedom as our pursuit, school leaders must employ an abolitionist struggle to communicate in ways that embody eight aims connected to the directness principle, explicitly humanizing the lived experiences of the recipients as being deeply impacted by whatever is being communicated. All eight aims do not have to be represented in every communication, but compromising any of the aims immediately places at risk the pursuit of freedom. The following eight abolitionist framing principles are intended to provide *all leaders*, markedly white leaders, at every level of leadership with a reference point that ensures, above all else, communication in crisis and heightened community moments does not sacrifice oppressed folx in the process.

Principle 1: Above All Else, Do No [More] Harm

Malcolm X, a critical voice in the emancipation history of Black folx, said,

> If you stick a knife in my back nine inches and pull it out six inches, that's not progress. If you pull it all the way out, that's not progress. The progress is healing the wound that the blow made … They won't even admit that the wound is there.[7]

At the core of abolitionist communication is the practice of attending to the wounds and traumas caused by crisis. Yet, in 1964, Malcolm underscored that in the grueling work of undoing the trauma of slavery in this nation, most American white folx had yet to admit the presence of the wound itself—structural oppression. And much the same, today, many white school leaders still have yet to admit that the wound—structural oppression, or even the knife, systemic racism—is there. In the spirit of the oath undertaken by physicians, abolitionist communication, above all else, should do no harm to the community. That is to say that school leaders in all communities, but particularly in Black, brown, indigenous, and oppressed communities, have a responsibility to do no harm; and for white school leaders, to do no more harm than what has been done. How is harm evaded? By acknowledging the presence of the wound *and* the knife that has contributed to consequential traumas plaguing communities of color, namely Black communities over the last 400-plus years. This nation has been home to systemic and structural oppression in sociopolitical, sociocultural, socioeconomic, and socioenvironmental contexts. Twisting the knife of racism, continually widening the wound, has been fatal to countless Black lives: those beaten and tortured on plantations, lynched as "strange fruit" on trees, viciously stricken by fire hoses and police dogs in the Jim Crow south, and blatantly murdered at the hands of the police state. Doing no harm is, minimally, *refusing to ignore the presence and consequences of racism and systemic oppression.*

Principle 2: Be Very Clear, It's Not about You

Our ethical commitment to abolitionist communication is rooted in the idea that what we say is for the advancement of communal consciousness. As such, abolitionist communication should, at all costs, avoid any moments of a "what about me?" individual consciousness from the leader. Any leader who centers a "what about me?" ethic instead of "what about us?" ethic is laying the groundwork for communication debauchery. Is this lack of self-focus fair, particularly when the leader is as impacted by the crisis as the community being led? Of course it is—communally conscious leaders must center the realities and needs of the community, at all costs including costs to self. In that sense, maintaining a communal, selfless ethic while communicating amidst crisis is analogous to communicating with a preschooler. When we communicate with a four-year old about a critical matter that impacts their life, their safety, and their future, i.e. "don't touch the stove or you'll get burned," it is *not* about us; we must get the point across clearly and boldly, *and* we must maintain vulnerability that demonstrates our humanity in order to ensure that the child is willing to trust what we're saying. And, to not only trust us this time, but to trust us the next time, because let's be immensely clear, there will be a next time. One of the fatal mistakes we often make in communicating with preschoolers is the same mistake we make in communicating during crises with adults: our focus in communication is self-centered and self-impacted.

Principle 3: Address the System and the Issues, Not People

Have you ever heard the phrase, "if you don't have anything nice to say it, don't say it at all?" Ignore that long-held wisdom when it relates to abolitionist communication—it serves no value. For abolitionist communicators, the criticality of our pursuit of freedom demands that we focus what we say on the issues we are addressing, not individual people, even if what we have to say fails the litmus test of niceness. While niceness is not the measurement of our communication, as teaching and learning leaders, we should avoid a threadbare approach of using crises and other heightened communal events to soley place blame on individual people. Focus, instead, on the system. Douglass' address to the Rochester Ladies' Anti-Slavery Society at Corinthian Hall included a roll-call of slave-holding individuals, many of whom we can assume would have been known, by name, affiliation, or relationship. But in the entirety of his address, he refutes the idea of individualizing the problem, knowing that the influence of a moral moment is in foregrounding the system underpinning the complicit, depraved morality of individuals. "There is not a nation on the earth guilty of practices more shocking and bloody than are the people of the United States, at this very hour." By focusing on the system and the issues, instead of the individual participants, Douglass' scorching critique of the unkept promises of the American democratic project has stood the test of time and continues to echo as a prophetic admonition against the lingering consequences of chattel slavery. No one single human in the history or current fabric of this nation, even the vilest human conceivable, is the sole embodiment of the protean power of American racism. *Only* the system is the culpable.

When we, as abolitionist communicators, minimize ourselves by addressing individuals, instead of the system, our complicity in individualism undermines the communal consciousness in the pursuit of freedom. Communicative critiques of people as individuals instead of people as conspirators within systemic oppression weaken the abolitionist process. While our communication should not exclusively indict individuals, neither should it attempt to justify, defend, or absolve individual conduct, particularly in a moment of crisis. Oppressed folx have borne the individualizing of moral crises, as an attempt to dislocate the stem of our plights and paucities—racism. Reflect on this two-part question: does your messaging critique structural practices and systemic policies, or does your messaging center individual complicity? If it messages individual complicity, how do you do the work of imaginative hope for a freedom framework, if you have only maintained an individual-specific message?

Principle 4: Abolition Is a Long-Term Strategy

Enslaved Africans arrived in this nation in 1619, and as you read these words today, Black folx are still in pursuit of the ideals of freedom, equity, and justice. Four hundred-plus years after the beginning of the Middle Passage, one-hundred and fifty-eight years after the signing of the *Emancipation Proclamation*, and fifty-six years after the passage of the Civil Rights Act of 1965, abolition is still an active process. That's why it is of the utmost importance that our communication prioritizes a long-term strategy to the pursuit of freedom. When we utilize short-term wins and immediate actions, we must not do so in sacrifice of the more tedious work of systemic, structural, and sustainable change. Is it a balancing act? Of course, it is. Are both fundamental? Of course, they are. But if we are deeply guided by our freedom framework where "slavery and prejudice, sin and sorrow in *every form* [individual and institutional], are unfelt and unknown," then we must recognize that our communication today lays groundwork for future revolution. Contemporary, history-changing protest movements like Black Lives Matter, DACA/Dreamers, #MeToo, climate change, and gun control are broadenings of a long-term, movement-building strategy of the sociocultural and sociopolitical protests in the 1960s and the enslaved rebellions of the 1800s. As such, short-term decisions in our teaching and learning community like organizational structures, title changes, salary adjustments, uniform policies, and racial equity statements must be situated within a more expansive, long-term strategy that abolishes systemic structures of oppression within teaching and learning.

For sixty-eight years following the 1896 *Plessy v. Ferguson* decision when the Supreme Court ruled that "separate but equal" facilities for Blacks and whites were, in fact, constitutional, Black and white folx remained diametrically unequal in the context of democratic participation and the fulfillment of American ideals. Even after the 1954 *Brown v. Board of Education* decision in Topeka, Kansas, when the Supreme Court ruled that "separate" was constitutionally and inherently unequal, Black folx maintained our status as unequal in this nation. It is why the civil rights movement for comprehensive reconstruction through legislation was critical, because it would serve as a long-term strategy for moving Black folx in the direction of freedom. From 1957 with the Eisenhower administration's first framing of civil right legislation, until congressional passing of the Civil Rights Act of 1964—which prohibits civil discrimination on the basis of race, color, religion, sex, or national origin, including prohibiting job description on the basis of race and sex—civil rights leaders and organizations like the Southern Christian Leadership Conference (SCLC), Congress on Racial Equality (CORE), and the Student Nonviolent Coordinating Committee (SNCC) recognized that short-term would not suffice. Pervasive and systemic oppression against Black folx would only be changed through long-term, sustainable legislative strategies. As abolitionist communicators, our burden is to lead our teaching and learning communities to disallow the sensationalism of immediacy, particularly in crises, to neglect our steadfast devotion to a comprehensive, long-term strategy inspired by an imagination that removes the limits of possibility in order to see freedom in a new way.

Principle 5: Words Are Never Just Words—Choose Wisely

Advancing meaningful, abolitionist communication, particularly in crisis, is a task of words—word choice, word meaning, word tone, and word context. We have already discussed how words, language, and rhetoric are meaningful, but beyond words creating meaning, words exist in an ether of context, history, translation, mood, appropriation, identity, and relationship to power. Consequently, the potency and influence of our communication are predicated on the story we create by strategically using words to construct, overhaul, and dismantle meaning. As abolitionist, a part of our responsibility in cultivating a communal consciousness of freedom is to *free* words and language from the grip of oppressive uses and subjugating meaning-making by framing *all of our words* within a freedom framework. By freeing words from oppression, we invite students within our teaching and learning community to free themselves from the devastating and traumatizing impact of exploited and maltreated rhetoric. Our students, teachers, staff, and families are listening to and reading every word we release, and therefore, it is not only crucial but also necessary that our communication uses person-first, human-always, inherently dignified language that supports freedom, justice, and equity, and not reinforce notions of stigma and pity that often surround our communication in the name of compassion and "feeling bad." You might be asking yourself—how do I go about ensuring that I am choosing words wisely? Here are two considerations to keep at the frontage of all communication—written and verbal.

First, humanely and correctly label identities and sociocultural statues. Humanely denotes that abolitionist communication should lead with emphasizing the inherent dignity of communities being discussed or addressed, thus focusing on our humanity. Any label identity and/or sociocultural status that reduces a community of individuals to a condition or behavior undermines the radical inclusion of a freedom framework. Instead of "ex-con" or "felon," which underscores criminal justice affiliation—without acknowledging the mass incarceration and prison industrial complex that disproportionately impacts Black folx—our communication should be "people with felony convictions," or "formerly incarcerated." In a sociocultural era where folx of color are progressively outnumbering white folx, a word like "minority," which denotes lesser or smaller than, carries an undermining connotation and contextual meaning; in its place, abolitionist communication should use "people of color" if in fact referencing *all* people of color, or it should use "Black people," "Latinx people," and the like for specific references. Similarly, the false gay and lesbian binary as the only categories for non-heterosexual identity is not only invalid but also rejects the expansive identities of queer folx in our nation. Thus, we have a responsibility as abolitionists to intentionally and purposefully honor the identities of people with non-heterosexual identities with words like "LGTBQIA people" or "people who identity as LGBTQIA," without using oppressive and callous jokes like "We might as well use the alphabet." As abolitionists, we vehemently reject any and all callousness of oppressed identity-based farce and mockery. Moreover, as leaders of public schools, which often, but not universally, have higher enrollment of families who are income insecure, caregivers between jobs, families facing economic barriers, families who are housing vulnerable, unhoused, or Section 8, (Housing Choice Voucher Program) participants, we must center those phrases as human-focused versus talking about folx within our teaching and learning communities as being "on welfare," "on food stamps," "poor," "struggling," and "disadvantaged." When we talk, instead, about the "under-resourcing" of families and communities, we are indicting a willfully neglectful system rather than imposing deficits onto directly impacted populations.

Second, and even more progressive in our pursuit of freedom, we must wholly abolish archaic, problematic, and characteristically offensive phrases, cultural idioms, analogies, *and* metaphors in order to communicate with clarity and directness. Growing up in the Midwest, wisdom was often communicated through analogies and metaphors; and as I continue to age, I become astonishingly more aware of how insulting and verbally abusive these metaphors are in our communication, particularly those rooted in a history of racism, ableism, and classism. Phrases like "turn a deaf ear" or "the blind leading the blind" or "master teacher" and a host of others not only cast a negative connotation on varying physical abilities and historical, racist positional power politics but also underscore dehumanization, which is contradistinctive to a freedom framework. People living with non-hearing and non-visible diverse physical abilities deserve more out of our communication than our tactless idioms. Even colloquial phrases like "leveling the playing field" and "do more with less" employ a competitive, individualistic, win-loss framing. This, while the task of freedom underscores the universal progress of all with a grounding belief that the American democratic project is only realized when there is *no* "playing" field, but only a place of equity. In a nation where our global economy is built on a premise of prosperity, abolitionist communication compels us to call America on that premise by rejecting a scarcity-based, competitive framing. We can critique economic inequity by naming it for what it is, without reinforcing oppressive, colloquial rhetoric.

Principle 6: Balance Problem and Possibility

As abolitionists, we are compelled to see and name the problem in our communication, which is at the root of our pursuit—dismantling the inherent and systemic problems that plague communal advancement for oppressed folx. Experiencing daily moments of a system that fails to center the very oppressed communities at the greatest risk of being neglect from participation in the ideals of the American project can often create a communicated sentiment of fatigue, by over-privileging all the problems in this country, and there is no shortage of problems to address. But as abolitionists, we must make an intentional decision to communicate the work of hope that we are called to lead our students in doing in response to the traumas plaguing their lives and communities. Mariame Kaba, an educator, prison abolitionist, and community organizer, contends that "hope is a discipline," in that it must be practiced as a habitual act if we are going to cultivate a consciousness to imagine possibility. In that sense, a freedom framing must be a balanced framing of problem and *predominantly* possibility—one that assumes our communal ability to address, strategize, and, ultimately, abolish any teaching and learning problem, oppression, or repression by exercising the discipline of hope. Emphasizing possibility as a deeply abolitionist practice counters oppression fatigue often experienced by teaching and learning leaders. In this state of fatigue, leaders experience such a barrage of sociocultural and sociopolitical injustices and inequities that leaders resign to apathy because of the perceived impossibility to abolish any of them.

However, we must not confuse possibility and positivity in this principle. An intentional, abolitionist use of possibility, grounded in hope, uses communally conscious strategies and tactics to address the intersectional barriers for oppressed folx regardless of the emotive impact of the strategies. That is to say, abolitionists are less concerned about the discipline of hope yielding positivity if it ultimately yields possibility. At the same time, abolitionists contend that, as our nation continues its expansion of freedom to be inclusive of all oppressed folx, it inherently yields a more hopeful nation, which in fact yields a more positive nation. In effect, hope produces its own positivity. As teaching and learning leaders, then, we must intentionally monitor the problem-to-possibility balance within our communication by asking ourselves a simple but significant question—where's the hope? Not a flaccid hope that solely looks to the future submissively, but a discipline of hope that looks to the future with a strategically synchronized effort that actualizes the human imagination of freedom.

Principle 7: Control for the Knowledge-To-Impact Ratio

Growing up, I spent many, many hours with my grandmother, Alma (affectionately known as, "Granny" or "Madea")—namely because I loved being at our church on Washington Avenue in St. Louis, where she spent the latter part of her life as our church sexton. In spending time with her, I noticed that she'd always tell the same story in multifarious ways, all dependent on to whom she was talking. The overarching premise was consistent, but the audience governed the level of detail, tone of speech, amount of inserted judgment, and moral evaluation of the story. When someone would die, which she always learned of before the hundreds of others who attended our church by proximity of her work, she'd tell me in a manner that was appropriate to a young, Black child as the audience. She'd say, "You know, Ms. So-and-So, don't ya'?" Uncomplicatedly, without much emotion in her voice, she'd say, "She died today." And that was the limit of the story she chose to share with me. But I noticed that when my mother would come to pick me up, the level of detail would increase considerably. My grandmother would say, "You know Ms. So-and-So died." Of course, my mother didn't know because she had been at work all day, but it was my grandmother's way of normalizing the heightened moment. She would then go on and tell my mother a few meaningful pieces of knowledge that contextualized the story, such as the longevity of the sickness, or the person who called the church as the informant, or any emerging details she had about the funeral services. Then, I noticed—as the nosey, young Black child that I was—if she was talking to one of her friends, the story took on a whole new level of productive value, with emotive one-liners, details completely immaterial to the main idea of the person dying, but details that made sense to making meaning of the relationships that existed between my grandmother, her friends, and the subject of the conversation. They were more impacted by the knowledge being received, and therefore merited (and potentially insisted on) details befitting the level of effect the knowledge had on their lived experiences. What differentiated our level of detail? Something I call, *knowledge-to-impact ratio*.

One of the most critical components of working through abolitionist communication in a freedom framework is how you communicate the issue at hand with the varying audiences within your teaching and learning community. How you go about differentiating your communication for the varying audiences within your community, and the way you determine the level of detail, tone of speech, amount of inserted judgment, and moral evaluation of what you're communicating, has the propensity to make or break how the community is positioned to move toward freedom. As a result, you must prioritize from immediate impact to secondary impact to tertiary impact, and then sequence your level of detail to respond correspondingly based on the proximity of impact to the issue itself. Ask yourself: who is *most* impacted by this particular moment and how do I communicate enough detail, with the right tenor and tone, and a clear moral evaluation so that those *most* impacted feel seen, understood, cared for, and held in this moment? By strategizing and framing your communication in the context of knowledge-to-impact, you control the narrative that the least-impacted—media, community partners, and so on—receive and thus keep the immediate teaching and learning community at the foreground of communication.

Principle 8: Give Credit to Folx of Color

Less than twenty-four hours after Bruce Tucker, a Black factory worker, was rolled into the Medical College of Virginia on May 24, 1968, white physicians removed him from life support and stole his still-beating heart, without informing his family, receiving their permission, or even crediting Tucker for the use of his heart when the story was disclosed.[8] It was stolen for a white heart transplant candidate, and it was only discovered because the funeral director, understanding the role of meaningful and influential knowledge for freedom sake, informed the family that the body had a missing organ. The injustice of involuntary organ appropriation, now deemed a federal crime, is but one of many grotesque, unjust, and oppressive appropriations (and sociopolitical heists) that have plagued Black and oppressed folx for decades, even hundreds of years. From the appropriation of Ethiopian servants' garments and performativity in the royal courts during the European Renaissance, to white performance of Blackface minstrelsy in the nineteenth century, to the appropriation of jazz, blues, gospel, and hip-hop from the 1920s up till now, to the mimicking of Black voice in oratorical cadence and rhythm in Protestant religious contexts, to models of justice movement-building and antiracist strategy produced by nonviolent organizations from the 1960s to now, Black folx have habitually been uncredited and under-credited for our social revolutions, cultural symbols, movement-building, contributions to American identity, the ways our bodies have been used and misused to advance this nation, and even our communication.

Too often, the abolitionist ideas and rhetoric being espoused by white leaders of teaching and learning communities are appropriated intellectual-justice capital from Black leaders, Latinx leaders, indigenous leaders, women non-white leaders, queer non-white leaders, and other oppressed folx without receiving the credit due for our words. This unpardonable practice of appropriation is oft defended by white leaders in the name of "they said it so much better than I could have." Too often, the rapid pace of communicating amidst crises, and the power dynamics of teaching and learning organizations where white leaders are the public representative, can instigate oppression by omission—omitting who and where ideas, concepts, motivations, and inspiration originated. By giving credit to folx of color in communication, white leaders embody an abolitionist framework of freedom by freeing folx of color to experience wider public visibility, wider opportunities for investments, and wider movement-building momentum. Ask yourself a question—am I giving credit where credit is due?

How to Actualize Abolitionist Communication

When crises are brewing, news headlines are increasing in volume, staff are clamoring to know how to proceed, students are digesting information faster than we are—mostly because of social media, and family are spreading real and created information as the rumor mill intensifies, I have no doubt that these eight principles will feel distant. In volatile, time-sensitive, fast-moving, and uncertain situations, like a global pandemic or a climatic disaster, as a school leader you must remember that all ears will be listening to what you communicate, how quickly you communicate, and how often you communicate. Even if you're still trying to understand the extent of the crisis and the implications it will have in your community, the depth of your honesty and vulnerability will determine your humanity. The coordination of how you communicate honest and vulnerability will determine your credibility. Here are the initial three abolitionist steps for how to actualize the communication principles with humanity and credibility.

Establish a Communications Team

Communicating as a group, unlike acting as a group, requires a more centralized communications approach. Not hierarchal, but centralized. These differences are more than semantics, but speak to the abolitionist spirit of how the school, network, district, or organization will communicate. When volatility and time-sensitivity are the background noise of communication, keep this in mind: *the fewer the voices, the clearer the message*. This communications team is not only formed to norm on what is being communicated but also to be the gatekeepers of principles. In a school-based context, these teams should ideally be no more than a handful, literally five people, and should at least consist of the principal (to be the primary voice and signature for all internal and external communiqué), an operations leader (to ensure that all the moving parts of communication make sense), and a social-emotional leader, e.g. a lead social worker or therapist (to ensure that radically human care is as critical as operations). Taking a triangulated approach to communication prevents any single leader from disregarding any of our communication principles, and promotes abolitionist accountability. You might be asking: *what does this communications team do?* In brief—it meets consistently (in crisis, daily!), creates and cross-references all information shared internally and externally, provides a weekly update or memo to all stakeholders (yes, *all* stakeholders!), and keeps the community focused on the agreed-upon and shared principles for acting.

Communicate with Students Daily

Students are our primary focus. *Digest that*. In crises, particularly ones that have economic implications, we can drift from acting and communicating with that truth in mind—students are our primary focus. As our primary focus, our abolitionist rhythms ground and guide that their well-being, humanity, joy, potential, hope, and freedom should be our aims. Want to know a not-so-secret secret? Students know what's happening in the world. By overhearing the news, eavesdropping on a phone call, checking their social media, scrolling their timelines, and talking with friends, our students are more informed than we often give them credit for. Hence, an abolitionist communication approach to actualize humanity and credibility with our students demands that we communicate with our students like knowledgeable global citizens. From the youngest to the oldest student we serve, our duty is to hold their fears, reassure their safety, and answer their questions. We owe it to them. Everyday (yes, every single day) during a crisis is a new invitation—through morning meetings, community circles, do now's, exit tickets, read alouds, center time, reflection prompts, questions of the day, discussion groups, fireside chats, brainwriting, think-pair-shares, concept mapping, chain notes, idea line ups, sketchnoting, empathy mapping, debates, and interactive demonstrations—to communicate and invent hope with our students as we all make sense and make meaning of what is going on in the world.

Communicate with Teachers Weekly

Students and their well-being, joy, and freedom are our primary focus. The way we keep students as the main thing is by recognizing and admitting that our teachers are the most crucial human capital to students being well, joyful, and free. In crisis, then, when teachers are confused and disenchanted, we risk students being confused and disenchanted. How do we avoid confusion? By communicating. How do we avoid disenchantment? By communicating. How do I know? Because early in my school leadership I used to hold to the belief that teachers wanted all the details, and would delay communicating until I had all the details. Hear me, I was wrong! In an abolitionist context where it is clear that freedom is our collective pursuit, details are imperative but not foremost. What, then, is foremost in communicating with teachers? Demystifying what's happening behind the curtain of leadership. As school leaders, we must remind ourselves that we have the privilege of flying between 30,000 feet and 1,000 feet, holding both views and everything in-between within our fund of knowledge. Teachers primarily fly at 1,000 feet with their eyes intensely focused on the classroom of students in their care. Therefore, as abolitionist leaders, we are accountable for reducing the mystery, alleviating their anxieties, and holding space for our teachers to make senses of all the pieces working in tandem. One systematic and reliable way to do this is to create a weekly communication method—email, official memo, videoconference, town hall, or company intranet—that teachers can regularly look toward, amidst the crisis, as a way to get a broader and wider view.

Communicate a Promise, Track the Promise, and Keep the Promise

In traditional business theory, there is probably no single, more quoted communication axiom as popular as "underpromise and overdeliver." But, in the abolitionist pursuit of freedom, this oft-repeated bit of advice has an oppressive undertone in that it assumes that folx need their expectations regulated. Folx, namely Black and brown and under-resourced folx, have the agency to regulate their own expectations, and it is our responsibility that when we communicate a promise that we are sure that we can keep that promise. In a nation where Black and brown folx have incessantly been made promises—from our forced arrival on these shores to the 40 acres and a mule at our "emancipation" to the voting rights acts of 1965—abolition demands that we, as school leaders and holders of power within communities, position ourselves on the right side of delivering on our promises. How do we do that? By delivering what we say we're going to deliver, when we say we're going to deliver it, and how we said we were going to deliver it. Delivering on all three fronts leads us to actualizing humanity and credibility. As a respectability principle, folx trust folx who do what they say they are going to do. For that reason, it is equally as abolitionist to utilize saying "no" versus yielding to the temptation of making unrealistic promises. Abolitionist teaching and learning communities that serve disproportionately more Black and brown and under-resourced students are communities that must do what they say they're going to do, no exceptions. In the words of a beloved mentor, "If you get that litle knot in your stomach as soon as you promise it, because you can see all the ways it might not happen, then dammit, don't promise it."

How do we hold ourselves accountable to keeping the promises we make as a communications team? Progress monitoring. As school leaders, we are familiar with progress monitoring language as critical to our response to intervention (RTI), which is a multi-step instructional technique to provide targeted support to students based on individual areas for growth. Likewise, in our promise making, we can use a progress monitoring framework by creating (and communicating) clear, measurable, accessible, and assessable goals that invite all stakeholders to track the realization of our promise. Only you, as the school leader, and your team know the best measurable data points based on the promises you make to stakeholders, but they should be explicit targets that anyone can comprehend. With a communicate-monitor-act system in place, school leaders (and communications teams) invite accountability to do what we say we are going to do. And in the moments when we communicate a promise that forecasting is showing that we will fail to keep, our successive action should be humility, which would compel being honest, explaining why we likely not meet that promise, and communicating a new promise, or asking for time to figure out what we will be able to accomplish.

At its heart, every teaching and learning community is built on, managed by, measured against, and trusted according to a series of communicated promises. From the safety of the building to the pedagogy in classrooms to the decision-making of school leaders, everything we do is grounded in the promises we communicate to students, families, teachers, and our community. When freedom is the aim of our collective pursuit, and humanity and credibility are our grounding communication goals, every promise has the opportunity to be kept.

Notes

1. Luthra, Anchal & Dahiya, Richa. (2015). "Effective leadership is all about communicating effectively: Connecting leadership and communication." *Internal Journal of Management & Business Studies*, Vol. 5, No. 3, 43–44.
2. Dyer, Justin Buckley (Ed). (2015). *American Soul: The Contested Legacy of the Declaration of Independence*. Lanham, MD: Rowman & Littlefield Publishers, 64.
3. Sinha, Manisha. (2016). *The Slave's Cause: A History of Abolition*. New Haven, CT: Yale University Press, 5.
4. Williams, John & Marsh, Kevin. (2017). *Strategic Communication*. London: Offspin Media, 33.

5. Williams & Marsh, 34.
6. Stevenson, Brenda (Ed). (1988). *The Journals of Charlotte Forten Grimké*. New York and Oxford: Oxford University Press, 85.
7. Ambar, Saladin. (2014). *Malcolm X at Oxford Union: Racial Politics in a Global Era*. New York and Oxford: Oxford University Press, 122.
8. Weisberger, Mindy. (2020). "Landmark transplant in 1960s Virginia performed with heart stolen from a Black man." *LiveScience*. Retrieved from https://www.livescience.com/the-organ-thieves-historic-heart-transplant.html.

7

Asking a Lot of All: Reimagining Accountability for the Sake of the Community

In both the Eastern and Western worlds, it is well known that many of the great spiritual teachers often used parables to convey the deeper truths of life. The generational fables within African traditional religions, parables of Jesus in the Gospels of Christian scriptures, the colorful stories of the Baal Shem Tov in Chasidic Judaism, and the mystic stories of Sri Ramakrishna Paramahamsa in Hinduism all capture this principle of profound meanings embedded in uncomplicated, simple, and human stories in which we are invited to see ourselves. Dated around 500 BCE, this parable from the ancient Indian subcontinent has come to be known as *the parable of the blind men and an elephant*:

> A group of blind men heard that a strange animal, called an elephant, had been brought to the town, but none of them were aware of its shape and form. Out of curiosity, they said: "We must inspect and know it by thought, of which we are capable." So, they sought it out, and when they found it they groped about it. In the case of the first

> person, whose landed on the trunk, said, "This being is like a drain pipe." For another one who hand reached its ear, it seemed like a kind of fan. As for another person, whose hand was upon its leg, said, "I perceive the shape of the elephant to be like a pillar." And in the case of the one who placed his hand upon its back said, "Indeed, this elephant is like a throne." Now, each of these presented a true aspect when he released what he had gained from experiencing the elephant. None of them had strayed from the true description of the elephant. Yet they fell short of fathoming the true appearance of the elephant.[1]

What happens to be one of the most well-worn, clichéd words in all sociocultural and sociopolitical circles, from education to medicine to engineering to artificial intelligence to social justice? *Accountability*. As a school leader, I have seen too often how the concept of accountability gets used, and mostly misused, in interpersonal power politics, organizational manipulations, and explicit racism aimed at forcing oppressed folx to follow a directed-agenda, formed and informed by systems of power, rather than co-creating a shared vision that yields mutual accountability for the oppressed and the oppressor, the led and the leader. Is the idea of co-creating a communally conscious accountability system increasingly difficult in a self-centered, isolationist nation? Of course it is. As our teaching and learning communities are rapidly descending into dysfunctional circles of personality-driven oppressive systems, emboldened white supremacy, and intersecting crises of economic downturns and public health botches, communal accountability is more than important than it has ever been. So how might we construct accountability in ways that help us live a vision of abolition, yielding a pursuit and actualization of freedom for all the oppressed folx in our teaching and learning communities?

To start, abolitionist accountability requires a lens through which we see our teaching and learning power constructs—the personal and positional—as an oversized, gargantuan system that demands us, in a pursuit of freedom, to see and make sense of the system as a whole. Like the wisdom of the parable, often our accountability systems are isolated and disjointed metrics that each present "a true aspect" of our work as teachers and leaders gained from and grounded in our experience. Yet, because we approach accountability through the narrowness of our individual lens, we "fall short of fathoming the true appearance" of what and who we are holding accountable. By seeing, constructing, and approaching accountability as a whole, we diminish the inclination to have a narrowed-vision that fights over elements of a system—a system by design that underserves all oppressed folx. Instead, we develop a broadened vision that sees accountability as the whole system being deconstructed and reconstructed with a higher, freer, more ethical standard. Abolition in this sense of being a lens by which to see the system as a whole requires an acknowledgment, and naming, of the identity/ies of the ones shaping, managing, and assessing accountability, which directly influences the level to which oppression and racism operate. Accountability itself, then, must be seen as a massive identity power politics at work.

Who Is Danielson?

When we initially started conversations about teacher accountability in my current role, we had to have a candid and reasonably uncomfortable conversation about whose standards we were using to hold teachers accountable for student outcomes, particularly outcomes that yield abolitionist thinking and work products. Like thousands of schools across the country and overseas, we utilized a modified version of the Framework for Teaching (FFT), colloquially called the Danielson Rubric, which is a research-based tool for teacher evaluation created by Charlotte Danielson. As we considered alternatives within the context of our abolitionist pursuit, at the core of that conversation was an unspoken, and yet very apparent, question—*who is Danielson?* Charlotte Danielson, a fifty-plus year educator who has taught grades from kindergarten to university, is a white-identifying woman. Does her whiteness inherently preclude her from developing an abolitionist accountability tool for teachers? No, not inherently. Should her whiteness be an invitation to pause and consider whether or not her evaluation tool aligns with our abolitionist rhythms? Without a doubt.

Here's what the Danielson Group, her company, had to say about the tool: "The Framework for Teaching provides a common language for instructional practice, as well as a philosophical approach to understanding and promoting great teaching and learning." The words we must interrogate are "common" and "great." We can both respect the objective of Danielson in cultivating a rubric, and critique that a rubric grounded and guided by commonality and greatness is not equivalently a rubric in pursuit of freedom. Because to design a rubric that attempts to *evaluate* great teaching (thus holding teachers accountable for executing it), we'd have to have a communally conscious understanding of what great means in the pursuit of freedom. Moreover, we'd have to agree that there are universally emancipating methods of teaching that apply to *all students*, regardless of the identities, experiences, resources, backgrounds, isms, and phobias that have formed and informed a student's life in the classroom and beyond. As a result, we found ourselves coming face-to-face with the reality that deconstructing and reconstructing the individual elements of Danielson failed the rhythms of abolition, as much as deconstructing and reconstructing accountability as a whole. That reality led to a different set of questions, including: *who are we holding accountable? What are we holding folx accountable to? What are we holding folx accountable for? Who's holding us accountable as leaders? What is worth measuring if freedom is our pursuit? What is worth abolishing if freedom is our pursuit?*

With that in mind, what if instead of thinking about the parable of the blind men and the elephant as one of moral relativism (as in religious philosophy), or limited mental models of perceptions (as in systems-thinking), or inclusive racial and cultural understandings (as in critical race theory), we thought about the parable as signifying the dangers of limited, singular-focus, or nonexistent accountability where folx are consumed by elements of a thing, thus neglecting the enormity of the thing itself. Obviously, none of the men in the parable was correct in their assessments, but they were also not incorrect, because each of them responded with the truth of their limited, narrowed context. Their contexts simply lacked complete accountability for the whole. Thus, if they had cultivated an approach by which to make sense and make meaning of the elephant, as a whole, it would have prevented them from quarreling within the community, because each of them would have recognized that they were engaging only an element of the whole.

Abolitionist accountability, then, is not only about having a lens to see the system as a whole, but also about having a lens to understand our human solidarity as oppressed folx intertwined in a larger system. Human solidarity as a practice of relational and mutual accountability is abolitionist in that it explicitly cultivates a communal consciousness that says that we are all within "an inescapable network of mutuality, tied in a single garment of destiny. Whatever affects one directly, affects all indirectly." Those words by Martin Luther King, Jr., should compel us to deconstruct experiencing the accountability process as what follows when we do *not meet, develop, or exceed* a set of behavioral criteria—metrics commonly used by performance rubrics. Instead, we should experience the accountability process as communally moving toward, or moving away from, the pursuit of freedom as embodied in the abolitionist rhythms. This is not easy, but it is necessary.

To actualize the abolitionist rhythms, then, we must define *accountability as the method, or methods, directed at ensuring that a system is doing what it was devised to do in the pursuit of freedom* from oppression and injustice, for the folx who move, live, and function within the system. As such, an effective accountability mechanism generates information for leaders within the teaching and learning community that can facilitate the abolition of oppressive practices and implicit biases that impede the freedom pursuit. In turn, the accountability mechanism will inevitably increase legitimacy for the teaching and learning community in the eyes of all the folx within that community and the place in which it is situated. Pragmatically, Lerner and Tetlock conducted an exhaustive analysis of accountability from a psychological perspective, and their review determined that all accountability is situated in four mechanisms—*presence*: simple awareness that someone else is watching; *identifiability*: expecting that an outcome will be personally attributable to the person; *reason-giving*: expecting that one will have, or need, to explain actions; and *evaluation*: assessing one's performance with particular rules and consequences.[2] At the same time, I would contend that there is something lacking within these four mechanisms, which fail to capture the communal consciousness of abolitionist accountability.

If you joined just any about professional learning community (PLC) meeting, faculty development meeting, or pre-/post-observation grade team meeting, you would probably find two indicators at the core of every approach to accountability. Regardless of the technological platform, feedback cycle, nationally respected rubric, or state-based professional learning standards template used, most school leaders are concentrating their accountability around two indicators—*collaboration and data-driven*. Collaboration is centered around the practices of shared lesson-planning, interdepartmental consultation, teacher-to-teacher co-creation, open idea-generation, and decentralized decision-making in teaching and culture decisions within the classroom. Meanwhile, data-driven practice mostly involves the use of big, linear, school-based formative and summative data—attendance, end of unit tests, interim assessments, state exams, PSATs, SATs, Regents examinations (in New York), suspensions, expulsions, amount of family communication, and so on—to collect and analyze information about students and processes; that information ideally helps school leaders and teachers make more strategic, evidence-based decisions. Against this backdrop of indicators, our failure to center humanity in teaching and learning accountability is distressing, but not at all shocking. The American teaching and learning paradigm continues to rely on a nineteenth-century model of mass industrialization.

Contrary to popular messaging, the United States is one of the least progressive, least advanced, and least democratic nations in our frequency of standardized testing, linear assessment instruments, and comprehensive examinations. Countries with robust, publicly funded education systems, along with some American cities in mostly densely populated urban metropolitans, have been utilizing performance tasks and portfolios as well as project-based investigations (which invite students to engage through multiple-modalities), and open-ended question narrative responses (which include multiple days for planning, drafting, and revising knowledge) as a form of learning accountability. What we need is a new approach, an abolitionist approach, not only to *accountability for student learning* but also to *accountability for adults in our teaching and learning communities.* Our existing models of accountability embody a unilateral power politics, without tapping the insights, knowledge, experiences, and agency of every human within our teaching and learning community. As a result, we need to imagine a new system of accountability, where school leaders and teachers, students and families, and community leaders work together to create communal accountability.

Transcendent Mechanisms—Levers that Are Bigger than Us

It has become apparent to me that we have allowed accountability, as a concept, to become so substandard, inhumane, and narcissistic that it is captured within the mechanisms of *presence*—thinking someone is watching; *identifiability*: thinking whatever happens will be attributed to you; *reason-giving*:

thinking you'll have to explain yourself; and *evaluation*: thinking you'll be assessed and then receive either rewards or consequences. How desolate a concept whose every driving mechanism ultimately centers individualism and the ego. What if accountability is driven by self-transcending mechanisms, a higher order of ideals and values, and a sense of communal abolition as the framework for holding one's self to a standard?

Monday, March 5, 2018 was a rainy afternoon with predicted thunderstorms, and I wasn't in much of a talking mood when I boarded a flight to New York City. I was attending the annual gathering of the institutional and individual members of the United Negro College Fund (UNCF). A mix of reflection, exhaustion, and anxiety about the weather contributed to my sullen disposition. As we reached climbing altitude, a quirkily charismatic, Midwestern (his accent betrayed him) millennial, Sam, attempted to strike up conversation. I quickly discovered that Sam was a Reform rabbi who dynamically lived between the tension of ancient and modern worlds. He abstains from most forms social media, though he finds wisdom from Twitter; and he observes the holiest rituals of Jewish Shabbat, but also happens to love Black gospel music and Beyoncé, which instantaneously increased my intrigue for conversation. In college, I often attended Shabbat and High Holy Day services when invited by Jewish friends, and my graduate education is in theological studies, so, needless to say, we had bounteous points of conversation. For the duration of the flight, we discussed the contemporary role of prayer, the dangers of white liberalism in social justice movements, and somehow arrived at a discussion about transcendent motivators of human behavior as a way to reclaim white participation in racial justice. Sam commented, "As someone who is drawn to justice movements, having been raised by activist parents, I often question whether my motivations are as pure as they should be … or could be."

When I asked how he would identify his motivations, he responded,

> God is watching how I treat my neighbors, and Black people in this country haven't always experienced white people as being neighborly. So, I guess I would say that part of me is trying to honor God, and the other part of me is trying to rewrite a narrative, or I guess redistribute the power I have to those who I know have lacked access to power, but I don't know if protesting and sermonizing and organizing is enough to redistribute power—honoring God feels transcendent, rewriting the narrative feels self-centered, and I have no clue whether or not attempting to redistribute power is transcendent, or just political language that centers me again.

It led us to talk about this notion of transcendent accountability as accountability that is bigger than us, and therefore, what it means to be accountable to further a justice claim or a freedom ideal without self-centeredness and egoism subverting the accountability. As we prepared to land, the aftermath of our conversation yielded three mechanisms of transcendent accountability that feel meaningfully germane—*redistributing power*, *prioritizing oppression*, and *esteeming humanity*. These transcendent mechanisms are merely thoughts for introspective consideration as a leader, and therefore should be seen as an invitation for you and those you lead to explore what motivates your accountability as you pursue an abolitionist approach and what transcendent accountability mechanisms you are leveraging in pursuit of freedom.

Redistributing Power

Abolitionist accountability in teaching and learning communities invites a transcendent mechanism of redistribution, which is committed to redistributing access to power, access to opportunity, and *access to access* (think about that!) at every level of the community, from teaching to operationalizing to leading. At a base level, the transcendence of redistribution as a form of accountability says that we are accountable *because we believe in a critical* examination, deconstruction, reimagination, and construction of equitable distribution in access, power, opportunity, title, decision-making, metric determination, and compensation. In fact, a redistributive accountability approach is committed to asking one's self if *every thought, word, and action* is rooted in an idea of decentering one's power in order to redistribute that power to oppressed folx.

In most of our teaching and learning communities, accountability is a power hoarding system in a top-down (vertical) power dynamic where those at the top—us, the school leaders—are evaluating and assessing those "on the ground"—teachers, staff, operations. With what you know about abolition, does that sound emancipating? Seldom, do we as leaders invite the ground to evaluate and assess our performance, which reinforces our power hoarding. Instead, an abolitionist redistribution of power yields top-down, bottom-up, and across/diagonal accountability where all stakeholders within the community are evaluating and assessing each other in our *communal* pursuit of freedom. If you had to answer at this very moment how students evaluate your leadership, would you be able to? Do you have clear and concise feedback from families on how the operations team is embodying an ethic of freedom and justice? These are only two examples of a larger reality, which is that we must know in and through various intersections how folx within the community evaluate our abolitionist pursuits.

The importance of redistributing power in and for accountability is critical when considering an abolitionist approach to education. School leaders (all leaders, and yes I mean all) must agree and clearly express a belief that power hoarding is contradictive to abolitionist accountability, and therefore give careful consideration on how to share power in accountability systems and processes. In order to do this, leaders must:

1. **Identify the specific and distinctive knowledge within every stakeholder group in the teaching and learning**

community relative to another stakeholder group (that is—what can students *alone* tell us about ourselves? What can teachers *alone* tell families about each other? What can families *alone* tell teachers about students? What can we *alone* tell teachers about families? What can teachers *alone* tell us about ourselves?)

2. **Organize an inclusive process and timeline of evaluation at multiple points through the year for joint, multidirectional accountability** (that is—a one-time, forty-five-minute, end-of-year evaluation is insufficient to assess the pursuit of freedom for every stakeholder group in a community)

3. **Cultivate investment in joint, multidirectional accountability by providing a clear and compelling *why* behind the expanded process and timeline** (that is—inviting stakeholder groups to hold each other accountable will likely be met with hesitance and resistance because let's be honest, who wants to have multiple groups of folx giving them feedback?)

Prioritizing Oppression

Would you agree that everything that matters to us in teaching and learning has a tendency to be treated as if it matters equally? Would you be willing to admit that in teaching and learning communities, the system often overrates the technical and pedagogical functions of our work and underrate the reparative and healing functions of our work? Can we say that we, as a collective, have a tendency to misperceive our measures of priority? In this sense, prioritizing work that unapologetically centers the reparative and healing and freeing work with students of color, particularly Black and brown students, is a transcendent mechanism of accountability. When one is committed to the mechanism of prioritization, every practice, policy, protocol, process, and program is filtered through this lens—does what I am doing restoratively and justly prioritize folx of color? In essence, how will what I am doing prioritize the conditions for students of color in this classroom, in this school, in this community, and in this world? As Gorski asserts, in teaching and learning communities, prioritizing all students' needs as a function of "equality—attending equally to everybody's interests—reproduces inequity."[3] In response, we must be accountable to prioritizing the interests of oppressed folx in our communities, not to other the identities of the folx themselves, but to abandon our assumptions that free folx and oppressed folx require an equal level of prioritization and institutional investment in our pursuit of freedom. If the free are already free, then, by prioritizing the free, we are guaranteeing access to more freedom, which is privilege; by prioritizing the oppressed, we are moving toward the freedom already secured by the free, which is abolition.

Esteeming Humanity

For Rabbi Sam, the most transcendent form of accountability was his belief that God had an expectation of esteeming all of humanity as our neighbors—a value, or principle, or commandment that is critical to Judeo-Christian ethics but that dates back to early Egyptian thought, reflecting the goddess Ma'at, in a story called, *The Eloquent Peasant*. For teaching and learning communities, all of us should connect esteeming all of humanity to our belief that the ideals of freedom, hope, imagination, and possibility—the fruitages of our work—are inherently accessible. This idea of esteeming humanity as accountability is, in fact, the highest order of transcendence in that when we recognize and value the inherent dignity of all folx within and beyond our communities, we are compelled to solely act in ways that demand and demonstrate dignity above all else. Calling forth the generational wisdom of family elders, raised in the throes of Mississippi in an era of sharecropping, I'd often hear one of them say, "If you don't do anything else, treat me like a human." It may seem like a low bar for accountability—humane treatment of all folx—yet treating Black students like human as a mechanism of accountability would compel a reexamining of every practice, policy, protocol, and process that animalizes, criminalizes, and dehumanizes the teaching and learning experience. As we do the technical and pedagogical work we have been called to do, esteeming humanity is our devotion to find our way back to ensuring that before we clarify learning goals, simplify the language of core standards, and identify criteria for success, we personify a radically human commitment to the dignity of every student.

A New Abolitionist Accountability—Belonging

As we contemplate innovating an abolitionist approach to accountability—a new, freeing way to participate in fulfilling one's duties and commitments to a teaching and learning community—we are compelled to think about a broader conception of accountability in respect to the abolitionist ideal of pursuing universal freedom for all people. This broader conception of centering freedom in our accountability process raises obvious preliminary questions, the same questions we wrestled with as we started imagining an abolitionist way. *Who are we holding accountable? What are we holding folx accountable to? What are we holding folx accountable for? Who's holding us accountable as leaders? What is worth measuring if freedom is our pursuit? What is worth abolishing if freedom is our pursuit?*

In order to begin answering these questions, we must postulate abolishing our current notions of power-positional politics in teaching and learning communities. This means we must abolish our reporting assumptions that students are "held" accountable by teachers, teachers are "held" accountable principals, principals are "held" accountable by a superintendent, and a superintendent is "held" accountable by a Board. Our use of "hold accountable" rhetoric perpetuates power politics language of Black bodies being "held" accountable through oppressive plantation hostility, Jim Crow policing, and hyper-violent arrests tactics during protests. This does not suggest that teaching and learning communities must completely abandon the individual-to-individual level of accountability, where a particular role is accountable to another. However, this does suggest that limiting accountability to these kinds of binaries through suppressive language and continuing false constructs that deliberately situate power are inherently incongruous with the aims of abolition. At the same time, we must constantly recognize and give voice to the longstanding institutional and structural imbalances to accountability that have been perpetuated within our teaching and learning communities since school integration. In this situation, certain people in leadership roles, often white, have exercised positional hegemony over certain people in non-leadership roles, often folx of color, namely Black folx. Against that backdrop, using an abolitionist imagination, what does it look like to abolish the concept of accountability in any structural sense and lean into cultivating a culture of belonging that does the work of accountability?

The idea of belonging as doing the work of accountability is grounded in a proactive approach that connectedness to others, and to communities, is core human motivation. Do you remember Abraham Maslow, the psychologist best known for creating the hierarchy of needs? He contended that as our innate needs are met—from the physiological to the esteem/ego—we culminate as self-actualized beings. After our physiological needs (food, water, rest) and our safety needs (security, safety), we arrive at the need he calls "belongingness." While there are sufficient definitions for belonging, in an abolitionist context it refers to a sense of feeling like a *seen, heard, and known* member of community—a human—and one that inherently matters to others within the community.

Belonging is innate, essential, and human. Belonging is being. What appealed to the enslaved that attempted escape? Belonging to the community of those who were free. What appealed to the enslaved that shunned attempts at escape? Belonging to the community of those who remained enslaved. At its heart, belonging is the realization of being a part of something larger than us. Because it is "so primal, we often try to acquire it by fitting in and by seeking approval, which are not only hollow substitutes for belonging, but often barriers to it."[4] In our communal pursuit of freedom, and ultimately, in the human experience, the absence of that sense of belonging creates a sense of alienation, disconnection, and disengagement. Alienation shuns accountability.

I am alone, or am I?
    / who cares what I do?
Dark, cold, frozen
Others in residence
Uninvited guests
    / murmuring about me, but not to me
I know them
They do not speak
Forced entry
Breaking and entering
They do not scare me
I belong to them
They belong to me
    / do they know that I exist?
Unclothed, ashamed
Invisible

I am still alone, I think
But not lonely
    / they are still here
Dark, cold, frozen
My throat is dry
Something within
I want to speak
Who to talk to?
    / who cares?
    / who sees?

/ who hears?
/ who knows?
Silence
It gets louder
Kidnapped by the sound
/ enslaved with no expectations
/ free to do what I want
/ alone, I think
No words
Just feelings
When will they stop talking?
/ to each other, and talk to me
/ when will they see me?
Uninvited guests
Stop talking
I want to belong
/ belong.

— Robert S. Harvey

As it is in our personal lives, it is in our teaching and learning lives that a sense of alienation will inevitably move us to leave a community where we are not seen, heard, known, nor matter. Conversely, when we feel that sense of belonging in our teaching and learning communities, our best selves emerge, and with our best selves come a sense of self-accountability that aligns us to the principles, values, and ideological commitments of the community. What we know to be true is that every teaching and learning community has an *identity and a communal consciousness*—a set of community marker and ideals—that ground the work and pursuits of that community. As abolitionists, our ultimate pursuit is freedom and the work we are grounded in is creating radically human classroom communities that yield emancipated, hopeful, and imaginative students. Thus, folx who are a part of our teaching and learning community and who feel a sense of belonging to our work and our pursuits will inherently commit to the work in ways that demonstrate how their individual identity aligns with our teaching and learning community identity. It is that alignment which creates a sense of belonging, and it is that sense of belonging which creates accountability.

A teaching and learning community full of folx who believe they belong within the community is a community full of folx who will feel self-compelled to be accountable to the principles, values, and ideological commitments of the community, and will therefore align their pedagogical and cultural practices, by any means necessary, to continue to belong. Consequently, when an individual identity does not align with principles, values, and ideological commitments of a community committed to abolitionism, it is the burden and responsibility of the school leader to guide that individual to a new journey in a community where they belong. Likewise, it is the responsibility of an abolitionist school leader to cultivate a sense of belonging where every practice, policy, process, and protocol points toward freedom, and therefore folx who are not conspirators, or aspiring conspirators, of freedom are averted from infiltrating the teaching and learning community. How does the aversion happen in a radically human way? By foregrounding experiences of vulnerability in the recruitment process—experiences that include questions, stories, and conversations that embody vulnerability about oppression, injustice, inequity, racism, and freedom. Experiences of vulnerability will either demonstrate a sense of alignment and belonging, or they will expose misalignment and alienation. And the emphasis should be placed on *storytelling*—the most ancient practice of teaching, learning, and community-building.

Do you want to learn if the folx in your teaching and learning community share a sense of belonging to the abolitionist pursuit of freedom? At every staff or faculty meeting, have a period of storytelling where you invite new voices—from the emerging to the experienced—to tell a story from the previous week or month about a meaningful moment with a student, family, co-conspirator, or school leader, and listen to the words they use in their story. If you hear words about "freedom," "opportunity," "community," "hope," "imagination," "joy," "resilience," "emancipation," "abolition," "racism," "justice," "equity," "equality," "oppression," "dignity," and "resistance," those folx likely feel a sense of belonging. If you fail to hear those words, or other words in the abolitionist rhythms, those are likely the folx who are or will struggle to hold themselves accountable to the transcendent mechanisms of the communal consciousness. Can these folx be cultivated into abolitionists? Of course. Do you have the capacity, as a leader, to do foster that cultivation? Only you know the answer to that. As school leaders, it is easy to drift into saviorism with the teachers and staff in our teaching and learning communities, assuming we have the capacity to infuse belonging into and pull abolition out of individuals. As a result, we often try to create an identity for people, and with people, which ultimately function as "hollow substitutes" for an actual sense of belonging. In that vein, to cultivate a culture of belonging, the first step is creating experiences of vulnerability. The second step, equally as critical, is to intentionally and regularly listen to stories of meaningful moments from the folx within your community, and center those stories that are embodiments of the abolitionist pursuit of freedom. As the third step, take periodic moments within your academic year to invite all the teachers and staff to individual conversations where you ask only one question in various iterations: how are you finding your sense of community, or how are you feeling connected to folx within the community, or how do you sense your state of belonging in this community, or how do you feel connected to our pursuit and values? Be transparent and forward about the fact that you are inviting each person in the community to answer that question and communicate a clear and compelling why for asking that question of all members within the community. The *why* is because, as a school committed to the abolition of all oppressed folx, the community has to be led and driven by folx who feel a passionately human, radically moral, but no less divine, communally conscious connection to the work;

not only to the work, but also a connection to the people and to the place.

A New Abolitionist Accountability—Freedom

In a different imagination—what does it look like in a new approach to be accountable to a set of rhythms, or ideals, versus being accountable to an individual, or a particular title? To the extent that teaching and learning communities hold on to and continue to organize accountability around a set of positional powers, similar accountability might be pursued if those in positional powers were held accountable to the rhythms of an abolitionist approach to education. Moreover, by centering the rhythms over individuals, humans become accountable to other humans, with less focus on performing responsibilities and more focus on actualizing freedom. In this sense, freedom is often the absent presence at the accountability table. Its exclusion is utterly problematic from an abolitionist perspective, particularly since the challenge of individuals being at table inherently brings biases and prejudices. The operative principle in the abolishment of accountability as we conventionally structure it is that humans, irrespective of their titles and access to power, would be accountable for fulfillment of their contributions to freedom within the community, and freedom in due regard to the rhythms guiding our abolitionist approach to communal consciousness. Much the same, community leaders, elected officials, individual donors, school board members, and institutional funders should be accountable for fulfilling their contributions to freedom, which is a contribution that transcends their financial contributions. Instead, the highest contributions of community leaders, effected officials, donors, and board members is the intrapersonal task of holding themselves accountable to the abolitionist rhythms of communal consciousness, and wrestling with the question—how does my participation with, and contributions to, this teaching and learning community advance those rhythms? Of course, pedagogical and cultural accountability (for school-based folx), plus financial and operational accountability (for governance folx), are *dimensions* of accountability, but they are neither exhaustive nor responsive to the inherent dignity of the humans at the table; thus they are less critical to the human task of accountability.

A natural consequence of a more human, freedom-focused accountability approach is a move from individualism and isolationism in accountability to inclusion and communalism. This freedom comes in the form of freeing previously oppressed, excluded, disengaged voices to take part in the accountability process, concerns that traditionally have avoided the positional power politics. Imagine students and families participating in the accountability of Board members by engaging the knowledge and complicity of the board members in pursuing freedom. Envision community stakeholders participating in the accountability of principals by probing the school leader's embodiment, communication, and development of abolitionist rhythms. Consider the possibility of students participating in the accountability of a charter network Superintendent or CEO by engaging that leader in questions about how they are pursuing a freedom framework, analyzing their communication, and challenging their presence and participation in classrooms. Visualize the communal impact of teachers participating in the accountability of colleagues through freedom observations whereby teachers use the abolitionist rhythms to mutually determine the impact of teaching in the lives of students. In effect, a human, freedom-focused accountability approach allows teaching and learning communities to be more influenced by the diverse ideas, perspectives, contributions, and sacrifices of a wider community of thinkers that, because of historically systemic oppression and structural binaries, fall outside of the purview of an individual or small-group process. One of the effects of allowing for more, broader voices in accountability is an increased awareness that the limited folx we engage in accountability of other folx within our communities often lack a broad, human experience of knowledge to effectively account for all the rhythms of an abolitionist approach. As such, abolitionist teaching and learning communities must increasingly listen to multiple voices to help actualize accountability for teachers, staff, and leaders.

Show and Tell—The Transparency of Accountability

What is freedom, if it's private? Related to the imagination and design of a new abolitionist accountability approach is the Achilles heel of teaching and learning communities: transparency, a growth area not exclusive to our communities, but endemic in all organizations that involve humans and information. That is to say, abolitionist accountability demands *show-and-tell*. One of the misconceptions we often rely on as school leaders to perpetuate hiddenness and obscurity in our accountability processes is that humans within our teaching and learning communities are uninterested in the goals, objectives, and embodiment of values of others within the community. But like toddlers and preschoolers, adults, including teachers, are particularly inquisitive, interested, and engaged in the accountability of other adults. As such, the quality of the relationship between transparency and accountability in teaching and learning communities depends significantly on *the purpose* of the transparency, the definition of it, and how the implementation of it occurs. Our responsibility as leaders is to co-create a working definition of transparency with other folx in our community. This initially demands acknowledging that, when teachers and staff ask for transparency, there are as many conceptions of transparency as the number of folx asking for it. For our sake, the starting point is being clear that the purpose of transparency, in relationship to accountability, is to ensure the pursuit of freedom for all of our students by improving teaching and learning that abolishes oppression and deconstructs positional power politics.

By having a communally informed starting point for *why—freedom*, the usual contested questions regarding transparency—how much information should be revealed, and what might be the costs of revealing information—has less influence, because information sharing is not seen as inherently harmful. Instead, transparency is seen and experienced by the teaching and learning community as a precondition for mutual accountability, because transparency is never unilateral, but is always bilateral. In practice, a leader never shares an aspect of accountability about teachers within the community without sharing an aspect of accountability about themselves first. Traditionally, the trove of accountability metrics for school leaders has remained locked away in hundred-page binders and central office databases, with only a handful of folx having the capacity, whether in accessibility or knowledge or tenacity, to find it or ask for it. But an abolitionist leader understands and accepts the emancipatory significance in preemptively making their accountability metrics available to all members of the teaching and learning community. While increased transparency and accountability by the school leader is admirable, it does not go far enough, because transparency with the community is not solely about pulling back the curtain and allowing folx to more closely see. It is also about calling on folx within the community to participate in shaping and improving the accountability system itself, and the metrics being used to structure that system.

In an assessment of the intersection of transparency and accountability in social systems, particularly the relationship between governments and citizens, Jonathan Fox concludes that the openness of information on its own does not make a community accountable. It is *only* when there is community answerability to the questions, concerns, and ideas of the folx within that community that there is an impact of transparency on accountability. As such, communities with the power to share existing information must also produce answers if it wants to consider itself transparent.[5] Allowing for more engagement and participation from those being led is abolitionist because it frees the school leader from harboring the false assumption that self-accountability is the full measure of accountability in communities of oppressed folx; and it invites the lived experiences, perspectives, and knowledge of other folx to participate in actualizing the work that brings life to the community.

Many folx, acutely Black folx and queer folx and Latinx folx, carry justified distrust of leadership in all aspects of our society. Consider, then, how you as a teaching and learning leader can start to reclaim a trust in the existential idea of leadership by sharing your goals, objectives, metrics, and performance indicators (qualitatively and quantitatively) to move the community forward toward freedom. Could you imagine any possibilities of trust restoration if you were to invite for teachers, staff, families, and even students to ask questions about your goals and objectives and metrics and performance indicators?

As we strategized our communal response to Covid-19, racial unrest, and economic downturn, I made a vulnerability request of the leaders within our network. Every summer, for the first two to three weeks leading up to the start of the academic year, we have what our organization calls *Build Days*—it's what many other districts and networks call Summer Institute, Summer In-Service, or Teacher Training in preparation to welcome students weren't in the form. As part of Build Days, all of our leaders review our Beginning-of-Year (BOY) goal-setting process with the folx they lead or manage in order to identify goals, objectives, action steps, individual growth measures, and in response, how their manager can support them in achieving all of the aforementioned. This is a mostly typical performance management process, though some of our indicators pursue an abolitionist ethic, such as antiracist pedagogical practice, non-conventional qualitative metrics, and community collaboration. While they reviewed the BOY process with teachers and staff, I requested that all of our network leaders—deputy superintendents, network director of operations and strategy, network directors of inclusive learning, and all of our principals—*publicly* share their goals with their teams that they'd already shared with me. I then requested that they engage an entire session during Build Days in which they, as leaders, intentionally centered those goals for questioning, discussion, deconstruction, modification, and even erasure, if necessary.

On the second day of Build Days, I had an opportunity to join a virtual session led by one of our elementary principals. Though only two years into her role as principal, she is an influential, freedom-pursuing, abolitionist-minded leader who thoughtfully navigates the identity politics of being Puerto Rican and Italian while leading a school of mostly Black and brown students. She walked through her goals with a team of mostly experienced teachers in addition to a cohort of nine new teaching residents entering education for the first time. While reading the chat, I found a comment that fully captured the intended aim of transparency and its distinctive trust-building role within a teaching and learning community—especially a community making sense and moving forward amidst a world of crises. The comment was from a teacher with more than fifteen years of experience in education, who had built a remarkable reputation as a literacy specialist with an exceptional propensity to take the youngest learners and partner with them to grow their love of and engagement with all things literacy. She commented,

> Thank you so much for sharing this with us! It was a lot of information, and really overwhelming, but I feel like I know what you are working on and thinking about, and that helps me to know where I should align my goals. Plus, it is so helpful to see how these align with the network's guiding pursuits of love, healing, knowledge, and results. You made that so clear in how you presented these, and it is makes it so clear what we will and will not focus on this year, which we all know is going to be incredibly challenging—for us, and our scholars. I hope we can come back to each goal and have more time with them in breakout groups or grade-teams, and unpack each one with more detail. Thanks again for sharing!

For a leader to inspire someone in the teaching and learning community to say, "… that helps me to know where I should align my goals" and "it is makes it so clear what we will and will not focus on this year" it rarely gets as magical as that. Not only does this underscore a sense of belonging, but it also emphasizes a sense of self-accountability driven by that sense of belonging and transparent knowlege-building.

As a teaching and learning leader, consider the following questions intrapersonally, and with the leadership team of your school community:

1. What are some examples of opaqueness in the accountability process and practices in our teaching and learning community, and who are the primary drivers of conserving that opaqueness?
2. What are communal risks of embracing a show-and-tell model of accountability that embodies transparency? Are there indicators within the accountability process that are particularly opaque in order to protect individual sentimentality? What are the structural, political, and leadership oppressions at work by not showing-and-telling accountability indicators?
3. How could a vocal and behavioral valuing of transparency in accountability, by us and other leaders in the community, result in a meaningful increase in a pursuit of freedom, or more shared authenticity of the barriers to pursuing freedom?
4. How does confidence in teaching and learning leadership change in response to the transparent openness of accountability data? If our communities could see our proximity—positively or adversely—to the abolitionist rhythms, how could it revolutionize the embodiment of authenticity and trust?

Reimagining accountability for the sake of the community may seem obvious, but it isn't. It demands *asking a lot of all*, which is often why teaching and learning leaders stray away from reimagining how we do and embody accountability, as to avoid the risks of asking a lot from folx within a community who are already stretched. But reimagining accountability in humanizing and transcendent ways that point toward belonging and freedom makes a difference—not only in the lives of the students we are called to impact, but also in the lives of the teachers and staff. In a world of crises, there is a great deal of distraction. Do not allow the distractions to force you to double-down on ineffectual, inhumane, and insipid mechanisms of accountability. With competing distractions, it seems it would be easier to accept our current versions of accountability. Only it isn't. Leading teaching and learning communities amidst intersectional crises is not a moment to waste assuming the easy route. This moment matters because it opens a world of possibility about how we think, talk, and do accountability. And how do we get better at accountability? Not by doing what we've always done, but by imagining what we have yet to do.

Notes

1. Trotter, Laurence W. (2020). *Seeing the Light through Black Death: Salvation in the African Savanna*. Bloomington, IN: Trafford Publishing.
2. Gill, Brian P., Lerner, Jennifer S., & Meosky, Paul. (2016). "Reimagining accountability in K-12 education: A behavioral science perspective." *HKS Faculty Research Working Paper Series*, 2.
3. Gorski, Paul. (2019). "Avoiding racial equity detours." *Educational Leadership,* April Issue, 60.
4. Brown, Brene. (2010). *The Gifts of Imperfection: Let Go of Who You Think You're Supposed to Be and Embrace Who You Are*. Center City, MN: Hazelden Publishing, 26.
5. Fox, Jonathan. (2007). "The uncertain relationship between transparency and accountability." *Development in Practice*, Vol. 17, No. 4–5, 667.

Conclusion: A New Way, a New World, a New Song

Late in the evening on a Friday night, we were sitting in the odorous street, eight feet from the sidewalk, adjacent to the First Avenue bike-lane going north. We were protected by a western red cedar barrier, eighteen inches wide, made of 2×4 slats, painted black, with potted flowers topping the barrier. Tables of two and four were each adorned with fresh, white linen napkins and an antique Vermont brass oil lamp to give the illusion of a Parisian milieu. We were not in Paris. We were in New York City, in Midtown East—in Turtle Bay, the headquartered neighborhood of the United Nations and the Chrysler Building. As the nation fumbled to recover from an unparalleled global pandemic and restaurants struggled to stay alive, nearly 10,000 restaurants, out of more than 25,000 across the city, set up outdoor seating. Half of our table anxiously had their backs to the oncoming traffic. The entire table resigned itself to the gleaming lights of cars speeding against yellow lights, the chiming bells of bikers frustrated by patrons waiting in the bike-lane with their miniature dogs, the crescendoing cries of a two-month-old, my godson, longing for his mother's breast, the periodic piercing of sirens as police vehicles sped up the avenue, and the intermittent discharge of exhaust from buses. We talked and laughed, occasionally gazing through the tinted windows of the restaurant—dimly lit, serene, empty—a reminder of times past. "Can I get you something other than water?" the waitress asked pleasantly, but muffled through her mask. We placed our orders with flummoxed faces as we made sense of this new normal of fine yet obscene dining, in the street, surrounded by the city.

"This is, uh, new," a friend remarked. "A new way, a new world. And with the city as our ambience, a new sound.

I suppose if restaurants can figure out how to reinvent themselves, the rest of us can do the same." I realized, listening to my friend, that her notion of "can do" provides an opportunity for inaction, or even retroaction, which, in turn, is a crucible for stagnancy, complacency, or only conceiving a new by mere force of all options being gone. "Must" and "ought," on the other hand, are functions of people who are unwilling to be forced into new, because must-people and ought-people experience the notion of new not as an optional, responsive act, but as a moral imperative. What differentiates an abolitionist from a community organizer, or an abolitionist from a justice advocate? I would contend that it is a passionately human, radically moral, but no less divine burden, a daily burden, to hope, imagine, and construct a new way, a new world, a new song.

Between us, of all the fears that imprison our consciousness as educators and leaders, within teaching and learning communities, it is the fear of imagining a new way, a new world, and a new sound that mostly goes unexplored and unconquered. In the delicacy of holding the emotional obscurity caused by newness, we rarely explore the notion of new, in new ways. When we approach injustice, or discern inequity, our half-hesitant response, from a place of benevolence, is oft one of sorrow, apology, and declaring how we wished it was another way. Rarely, if ever, do our approaches with injustice compel our teaching and learning communities to ask, how would it look if there was a new way and a new world? We seldom ask, not out of fear of imagining—but out of fear of not actualizing the imagination, or out of overwhelm of not knowing where to begin to actualize the imagination. We turn aside that question, not out of fear of what it could be—but out of fear of who we'd have to become, or out of fear of not knowing who we'd become. We render void the wondering, not out of a fear of all things being made new—but out of a fear that we, too, would have to be made new.

One hundred and fifty-eight years after Lincoln declared, "all persons held as slaves within any State or designated part of a State, the people whereof shall then be in rebellion against the

United States, shall be then, thenceforward, and forever free," we still await a new way, a new world, and a new sound. This nation, our nation, has not yet found a new way from the distorted sins of its inception. Much the same, our public education system has not yet found a new way from the distorted sins of its inception. And for those of us complicit in its systems, we have yet to find our new way. Whatever good may have come from the decisions of Congress, the Supreme Court, and the pen of the presidency—in an effort to invite a newness for all—we have been bittered by reincarnated, morally palatable structures, relics of a so-called emancipated past. Here we are, in the throes of the twenty-first century, with wars and rumors of wars, a bigoted resurgence of organized white supremacy in the public domain, a lower-low of villainous political jesters, and a decline of economic advancement through rising unemployment. In education, we are still contending with the fallout of legislative propositions such as No Child Left Behind and Every Student Succeeds, both of which are contradicted by the unconscionable truth that our nation has not only left children behind, our nation is not engaging children; and not only is every student not succeeding, our nation has forecasted their lack of success by building jails and prisons.

The history, economics, and politics of the American classroom are full of stratification, struggle, and self-reliance—a human longing to exist within community, while using the community to seek and secure a better individual self. In this longing, the student is neither the focus nor the subject, but instead, is socialized to become an unconscious conspirator of capitalist individualism, unknowingly complicit in a survival of the fittest. The student, then, learns of and experiences the classroom, community, the nation, and the world not as an invitation for building a radically new way of social equity and communal reliance, but as a crucible of compliance bordered on all sides by fear and injustice, seeing neighbors as "the other." Whether conscious or not of the curse of whiteness and the smog of capitalist individualism, many of our students maintain a hope unseen, unheard, and unfelt that a new way is possible for/within all.

Hope, then, is the beginning of our striving toward a new way, a new world—and even a new witness. This new witness is a sound. Not in a literal sense, but a sound as a vibration of consciousness that reverberates as we move about the classroom, the community, the nation, and the world. But what does it mean for a student to hope if those of us who are curators of the classroom, conspirators of communal consciousness, and custodians of teaching and learning are in fear of what hope produces? For those who are in our care, we must escape the stronghold of our fear of new—and flee the shadow of the powerful who stand to gain with the survival of the system as it is. These escapes, as herculean as they may seem for educators and leaders, are menial relative to the ways in which our students must escape an oppressive worldview where "the other" is seen as competition in pre-fixed fight. Throughout the history and politics of the American classrooms, a new way and a new world only comes as the curse of whiteness grows weary of its own cadence, and succumbs by implosion, as it gives life to a new rhythm of the curse—sometimes dual rhythms contending, with whiteness lacking cognizance of its own syncopation. There, as the new rhythm of whiteness emerges, Black students and brown students and queer students and undocumented students are told to absorb this syncopated sound. But those of us who are abolitionists must guide our students in resisting the absorption, in order to create, listen, and walk to the rhythm of a new drum, a new beat, a new pace—one absent of oppression.

Yet it is fearsome to hope for a new rhythm and a new way, a sound that has yet been heard, but has been longed for by the ages. Hence, the double-aimed struggle of the student—namely the Black and brown ones—on the one hand is to attune an ear to whiteness as a matter of understanding its rhythm in the world, and on the other hand to listen as only oppressed folx can listen: with an ear to the cries of those whose tears are a bloodied symphonic of passionately human, radically moral, but no less divine possibilities. By holding in tension this double-aimed struggle of two unreconciled rhythms, the student embodies the knowledge necessary to pursue a new sound; and if a new sound is indiscoverable, one is made. Our role as educators and leaders is to make space for this pursuit in our classrooms, without fear, without contempt, without limits, without prejudices, and without the need to satisfy our own individualism. "Making space" may even be the wrong notion, since it yields agency of the new way to us, as adults, permitting students space to hope, to create—space that is not ours to give, nor to police. And why not? Because a new way, a new world, and a new sound is only within the agency of the one who must walk the new way, custodian the new world, and listen to the new sound. Thus, our burden as leaders in teaching and learning communities is using our hope to imagine and create a new way of relinquishing our classroom power, a new world where students are the subject of all that we say, think, and do, and a new sound of hymnic justice.

These things—hoping, imagining, and creating a new way, a new world, and a new song—should light fire within the deepest parts of our educational soul. New as an embodiment, as a being ought to compel you, as it compels me, to conduct a daily self-interrogation and endeavor to pursue it by any means necessary. And when you find yourself within communities, systems, or structures that oppress new ways, new worlds, and new songs, refuse to be overcome by fear. Refuse to be complicit in despairing the hope and imagination of the young souls within your care. Will you be found guilty of hope, or guilty of despair? Will you be indicted on charges of pursuing a new way, or will you be indicted on the grounds of constraining new? Where will you find yourself amongst the community—passionately human, radically moral, but no less divine? Or, passionately callous, radically depraved, but no less evil? In your teaching and learning community, system, organization, network, or district, you may be few, but you are crucial to the pursuit of a new way. It is true, the path less traveled, oft-lacking esteem and distinction, is the path most necessary. As you prepare to close this book, cast your eyes about and look as deep as you can into the eyes of the Black students and brown students and queer students and undocumented students, as deep as you can see. The glimmer you see in their eyes is a foretelling of all the new that is possible in the world. Do not ignore it, waste it, or, even worse, ravage it. See it, name it, and ignite it. Even now, against a wearied and dogged path of outworn ways in our classrooms, and in our teaching and learning, we must hope that a new way is possible. And because we can look in their eyes, it is possible—whether by our doing, or the earth's.

In pursuit of a new way, a new world, and a new song.